What readers are saying about
Pragmatic Version Control...

"This book gave me a boatload of ideas for improving my use of CVS. Recipes with rationale and examples help me do the thing I'm worst at: getting started. Why didn't you write this 10 years ago and mail me a copy!"

▶ **Mike Stok,** Senior Software Developer,
Exegenix Research Inc.

"An excellent introduction for folks who haven't used CVS. Dave Thomas and Andy Hunt are at their usual best."

▶ **Andrew C. Oliver,** founder of Apache POI,
SuperLink Software, Inc.

"I've been using CVS for years and I've learned a LOT! It's not only good, it's important to the software industry. This book makes arcane magic understandable to the "normal" developer."

▶ **Will Gwaltney,** Development Tester,
SAS Institute

"This is an excellent book; any programmer who hasn't even heard of version control will be able to pick up all the skills necessary to use version control and be productive. I absolutely love the way the book is written. The use of scenarios to explain every example and concept just works perfectly, and best practices are included in all of the chapters."

▶ **Vinny Carpenter,** Enterprise Architect

Pragmatic Version Control

with CVS

Pragmatic Version Control

with CVS

Dave Thomas

Andy Hunt

The Pragmatic Bookshelf

Raleigh, North Carolina Dallas, Texas

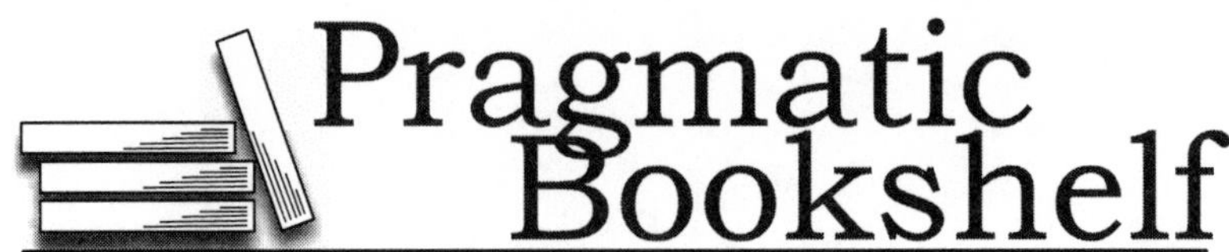

Our Pragmatic courses, workshops and other products can help you and your team create better software and have more fun. For more information, as well as the latest Pragmatic titles, please visit us at:

`http://www.pragmaticprogrammer.com`

Printed in the United States of America.

ISBN 0-9745140-0-4

Printed on acid-free paper with 85% recycled, 30% post-consumer content.

Third printing, May 2004

Version: 2004-4-22

Contents

About the Starter Kit

Our first book, *The Pragmatic Programmer: From Journeyman to Master*, is a widely-acclaimed overview of practical topics in modern software development. Since it was first published in 1999, many people have asked us about follow-on books, or sequels. We'll get around to that. But first, we thought we'd go back and offer a *prequel* of sorts.

Over the years, we've found that many of our pragmatic readers who are just starting out need a helping hand to get their development infrastructure in place, so they can begin forming good habits early. Many of our more advanced pragmatic readers understand these topics thoroughly, but need help convincing and educating the rest of their team or organization. We think we've got something that can help.

The *Pragmatic Starter Kit* is a three-volume set that covers the essential basics for modern software development. These volumes include the practices, tools, and philosophies that you need to get a team up and running and super-productive. Armed with this knowledge, you and your team can adopt good habits easily and enjoy the safety and comfort of a well-established "safety net" for your project.

This volume, *Pragmatic Version Control*, describes how to use version control as the cornerstone of a project. A project without version control is like a word processor without an UNDO button: the more text you enter, the more expensive a mistake will be. Pragmatic Version Control shows you how to use version control systems effectively, with all the benefits and safety but without crippling bureaucracy or lengthy, tedious procedures.

Volume II, *Pragmatic Unit Testing*, discusses how to do effective unit testing. Unit testing is an essential technique as it provides real-world, real-time feedback for developers as we write code. Many developers misunderstand unit testing, and don't realize that it makes *our* jobs as developers easier. There are two versions of this volume, one based on JUnit (for Java), the other based on NUnit (for C#).

Volume III *Pragmatic Automation*,[1] covers the essential practices and technologies needed to automate your code's build, test, and release procedures. Few projects suffer from having too much time on their hands, so Pragmatic Automation will show you how to get the computer to do more of the mundane tasks by itself, freeing you to concentrate on the more interesting—and difficult—challenges.

These books are created in the same approachable style as our first book, and address specific needs and problems that you face in the trenches every day. But these aren't dummy-level books that only give you part of the picture; they'll give you enough understanding that you'll be able to invent your own solutions to the novel problems you face that we *haven't* addressed specifically.

For up-to-date information on these and other books, as well as related pragmatic resources for developers and managers, please visit us on the web at:

`http://www.pragmaticprogrammer.com`

Thanks, and remember to make it fun!

[1]Expected to be published in 2004.

Preface

When done right, version control is like breathing; you just don't notice doing it, but it keeps your project alive. However, during our travels to teams around the world, we've noticed something: most of them aren't doing version control right (and many aren't doing it at all).

There are many reasons for this; when pushed most teams complain that version control is just too complex. They get the basics, checking stuff in to and out of some central repository, but when the time comes to create a release, or when they need to handle third-party code, things start getting out of hand. Frustrated, the team either stops using version control, or they bog themselves down with page after page of obscure procedures.

It needn't be that way. In this book we show how just a handful of basic recipes can be used to get 90% of the benefit from a version control system. Following these recipes, teams will start enjoying the benefits of version control immediately.

Your continuing feedback is very important to us. To report errors, omissions, or suggestions please visit our web site.[2]

[2]`http://www.pragmaticprogrammer.com/sk/vc/feedback.html`

Typographic Conventions

italic font	Indicates terms that are being defined, or borrowed from another language.
`computer font`	Computer stuff (file names, terminal sessions, commands, and so on).
	A warning that this material is more advanced, and can safely be skipped on your first reading.
	"Joe the Developer," our cartoon friend, asks a related question that you may find useful.
`-d` ⇒ Destination	An *aide-memoir* for a command option (in this case `-d`).

Acknowledgments

One of the joys of writing a book is that you get to ask friends to review the drafts. One of the surprises is that they agree to do it. We'd especially like to thank Steve Berczuk, Vinny Carpenter, Will Gwaltney, Volker Klaerchen, Krista Knight, Andy Oliver, Jared Richardson, and Mike Stok for all their useful comments and suggestions.

Dave Thomas and *Andy Hunt*
October, 2003
`pragprog@pragmaticprogrammer.com`

Chapter 1

Introduction

This book tells you how to improve the effectiveness of your software development process using version control.

Version Control, sometimes called source code control, is the first leg of our project support tripod. We view the use of version control as mandatory on all projects.

Version control offers many advantages to both teams and individuals.

- It gives the team a project-wide *undo* button; nothing is final, and mistakes are easily rolled back. Imagine you're using the world's most sophisticated word processor. It has every function imaginable, except one. For some reason, they forgot to add support for a DELETE key. Think how carefully and slowly you'd have to type, particularly as you got near the end of a large document. One mistake, and you'd have to start over. It's the same with version control; having the ability to go back an hour, a day, or a week frees your team to work quickly, confident that they have a way of fixing mistakes.
- It allows multiple developers to work on the same code base in a controlled manner. The team no longer loses changes when someone overwrites the edits made by another team member.
- The version control system keeps a record of the changes made over time. If you come across some "surprising

code," it's easy to find out who made the change, when, and (with any luck) why.

- A version control system allows you to support multiple releases of your software at the same time as you continue with the main line of development. With a version control system, there's no longer a need for the team to stop work during a *code freeze* just before release.
- Version control is a project-wide *time machine*, allowing you to dial in a date and see exactly what the project looked like on that date. This is useful for research, but it is essential for going back and regenerating prior releases for customers with problems.

This book focuses on version control from a project perspective. Rather than simply listing the commands available in a version control system, we instead look at the tasks we need in a successful project, and then see how a version control system can help.

How does version control work in practice? Let's start with a small story....

1.1 Version Control in Action

Fred rolls into the office eager to continue working on the new Orinoco book ordering system. (Why Orinoco? Fred's company uses the names of rivers for all internal projects.) After getting his first cup of coffee, Fred updates his local copy of the project's source code with the latest versions from the central version control system. In the log that lists the updated files, he notices that Wilma has changed code in the basic Orders class. Fred gets worried that this change might affect his work, but today Wilma is off at the client's site, installing the latest release, so he can't ask her directly. Instead, Fred asks the version control system to display the notes associated with the change to Orders. Wilma's comment does little to reassure him:

```
* Added new deliveryPreferences field to the Order class
```

To find out what's going on, he goes back to the version control system and asks to see the actual changes made to the source file. He notes that Wilma has added a couple of instance variables, but they are set to default values, and nothing seems to change them. This might well be a problem in the future, but it is nothing that will stop him today, so Fred continues working.

As he works on his code, Fred adds a new class and a couple of test classes to the system. Fred adds the names of the files he creates to the version control system as he creates them; the files themselves won't be added until he commits his changes, but adding their names now means he won't forget to add them later.

A couple of hours into the day, Fred has completed the first part of some new functionality. It passes its tests, and it won't affect anything in the rest of the system, so he decides to check it all in to the version control system, making it available to the rest of the team. Over the years, Fred has found that checking in and out frequently is more convenient than leaving it for days: it's a lot easier to reconcile the occasional conflict if you only have to worry about a couple of files, rather than a week's worth of changes from the whole team.

Why You Should Never Answer the Phone

Just as Fred's about to start the next round of coding, his phone rings. It's Wilma, calling from the client's site. It looks like there's a bug in the release she's installing: printed invoices are not calculating sales tax on shipping amounts. The client is going ballistic, and they need a fix now.

Unless You Use Version Control...

Fred double checks the name of the release with Wilma, then tells the version control system to check out all the files in that version of the software. He puts it in a temporary directory on his PC, as he intends to delete it after he finishes the work. He now has two copies of the system's source code on his computer, the mainline and the version released to the client. Because he's about to fix a bug, he tells the version control system to tag his source code with a label. (He'll add another tag when he's fixed the bug. These tags act as flags you leave behind to mark significant points in the development. By using consistently named tags before and after he makes the change, other folks in his team will be able to see exactly what changed should they look at it later on.)

In order to isolate the problem, Fred first writes a test. Sure enough, it looks like no one ever checked the sales tax calculation when shipping was involved, because his test immediately shows the problem. (Fred makes a note to raise this during this iteration's review meeting; this is something that should never have gone out the door). Sighing, Fred adds the line of code that adds shipping in to the taxable total, compiles, and checks that his test passes. He reruns the whole test suite as a quick sanity test and checks the fixed code back into the central version control system. Finally, he adds a tag to the release branch indicating that the bug is fixed. He sends a note off to QA, who are responsible for shipping emergency releases to the client. Using his tag, they'll be able to instruct the build system to produce a delivery disk which includes his fix. Fred then phones Wilma back and tells her that the fix is in the hands of QA and should be with her soon.

Having finished with this little distraction, Fred removes the source for the released code from his local machine: no point in cluttering things up, and the changes he's made are safely tucked back into the central server. He then gets to wondering: is the sales tax bug that he found in the released code also present in the current development version? The quickest way to check is to add the test he wrote in the released version into the development test suite. He tells the version control system to merge that particular change in the release branch into the appropriate file in the development copy. The merge process takes whatever changes were made to the release files and makes the same changes to development version. When he runs the tests, his new test fails: the bug is indeed present. He then moves his fix from the release branch into the development version. (He doesn't need the release branch's code on his machine to do any of this; all the changes are being fetched from the central version control system.) Once he's got the tests all running again, he commits this change back in version control system. That's one less bug that'll bite the team next time.

Crisis over, Fred gets back to working on his own tasks for the day. He spends a happy afternoon writing tests and code, and toward the end of the day decides he's done. While he's been working, other folks in his team have also been making changes, so he uses the version control system to take their work and apply it his local copy of the source. He runs the tests one last time, then checks his changes back in, ready to start work the next day.

Tomorrow...

Unfortunately, the next day brings its own surprises. Overnight Fred's central heating finally gave up the ghost. As Fred lives in Minnesota, and as it's February, this isn't something to be taken lightly. Fred calls in to work to say he'll be out most of the day waiting for the repair folks to arrive.

However, that doesn't mean he has to stop work. Accessing his office network using a secure connection over the public Internet, Fred checks out the latest development code on to his laptop. Because he checked in before he went home the previous night, everything is there and up to date. He continues to work at home, wrapped in a blanket and sitting by the fire. Before he stops for the day he checks his changes in from the laptop so they'll be available to him at work the next day. Life is good (except for the heating repair bill).

Story-book Projects

The correct use of version control on Fred and Wilma's project was pretty unobtrusive, but it gave them control and helped them communicate, even when Wilma was miles away. Fred could research changes made to code and apply a bug fix to multiple releases of their application. Their version control system supports offline work, so Fred gained a degree of location independence: he could work from home during his heating problems. Because they had version control in place (and they knew how to use it), Fred and Wilma dealt with a number of project emergencies without experiencing that panic that so often characterizes our response to the unexpected.

Using version control gave Fred and Wilma the control and the flexibility to deal with the vagaries of the real world. That's what this book is all about.

1.2 Roadmap

The next chapter, *What Is Version Control?*, is an introduction to the concepts and terminology of version control systems. There are many version control systems to choose from. In this book we're going to focus on the freely available CVS; on a day-to-day basis, CVS is probably the most widely used version control system.

Chapter 3, *Getting Started with CVS*, is a tutorial introduction to using CVS. The remainder of the book is a set of recipes for using CVS in projects. This section is divided into six chapters, each containing a number of recipes:

- Different ways of connecting to CVS.
- Common CVS commands.
- Using tags and branches to handle releases and experimental code.
- Creating a project.
- Creating submodules.
- Handling third-party code.

We end with an appendix summarizing all of the recipes and an appendix containing a brief list of other resources, along with a bibliography.

Chapter 2

What Is Version Control?

A version control system is a place to store all the various revisions of the stuff you write while developing an application. They're basically very simple systems. Unfortunately, over the years, various people have started using different terms for the various components of version control. And this can lead to confusion. So let's start off by defining some of the terms that *we'll* be using.

2.1 The Repository

You may have noticed that we wimped out; we said that, "a version control system is a place to store... the stuff you write," but we never said exactly where all this stuff is stored. In fact, it all goes in the *repository*.

In almost all version control systems, the repository is a central place that holds the master copy of all versions of your project's files. Some version control systems use a database as the repository, some use regular files, and some use a combination of the two. Either way, the repository is clearly a pivotal component of your version control strategy. You need it sitting on a safe, secure, and reliable machine. And it should go without saying that it needs to get backed up regularly. *repository*

In the old days, the repository and all its users had to share a machine (or at least share a filesystem). This turns out to be fairly limiting; it was hard to have developers working at

Different Flavors of Networked Access

The writers of version control systems sometimes have different definitions of what "networked" means. For some, it means accessing the files in a repository over shared network drives (such as Windows shares or NFS mounts). For others it means having a client-server architecture, where clients interact with server repositories over a network. Both can work (although the former is hard to design correctly if the underlying file-sharing mechanism doesn't support locking reliably). However, you may find that deployment and security issues dictate which systems you can use.

If a version control system needs access to shared drives, and you need to access it from outside your internal network, then you'll need to make sure that your organization allows you to access the data this way. Virtual Private Network (VPN) packages allow this kind of secure access, but not all companies run VPNs.

CVS uses the client-server model for remote access.

different sites, or working on different kinds of machines or operating systems. As a result, most version control systems today support networked operation; as a developer you can access the repository over a network, with the repository acting as a server and the version control tools acting as clients. This is tremendously enabling. It doesn't matter where the developers are; as long as they can connect over a network to the repository, they can access all the project's code and its history. And they can do it securely; you can even use the Internet to access your repository without sharing your precious source code with a nosy competitor. Andy and I regularly access our source code over the Internet when we're on the road.

This does lead to an interesting question, though. What happens if you need to do development, but you don't have a network connection to your repository? The simple answer is, "it depends." Some version control systems are designed solely for use while connected to the repository; it is assumed that you'll always be online, and that you won't be able to change source code without first contacting the central repository. Other systems are more lenient. The CVS system, which we use for our examples in this book, is one of the latter. We can edit away on our laptops at 35,000 feet, and then resynchronize the changes when we get to our hotel rooms. This online/offline issue is a crucial one when choosing a version control system; make sure that whatever product you choose supports your style of working.

2.2 What Should We Store?

All the things in your project are stored in the repository. But what exactly are the *things* we're talking about?

Well, you obviously need program source files to build your project: the Java, or C#, or VB, or whatever language you're using to write your application. In fact, some folks think that this source code is such an important component of version control that they use the term "Source Code Control Systems."

The source code is certainly important, but many people make the mistake of forgetting all the other things that need to be stored under version control. For example, if you're a Java programmer, you may use the Ant tool to compile your source. Ant uses a script, normally called `build.xml`, to control what it does. This script is part of the build process; without it you can't build the application, so it should be stored in the version control system.

Similarly, many projects use metadata to drive their configuration. This metadata should be in the repository too. So should any scripts you use to create a release CD, test data used by QA, and so on.

In fact, there's an easy test when it comes to deciding what goes in and what stays out. Simply ask yourself "if we didn't have an up to date version of *x*, could we build and deliver our application?" If the answer is "no," then *x* should be in the repository.

Joe Asks...

What About Generated Artifacts?

If we store all the things needed to build the project, does that mean that we should also be storing all the generated files? For example, we might run JavaDoc to generate the API documentation for our source tree. Should that documentation be stored in the version control system's repository?

The simple answer is "no." If a generated file can be reconstituted from other files, then storing it is simply duplication. Why is this duplication bad? It isn't because we're worried about wasting disk space. It's because we don't want things to get out of step. If we store the source and the documentation, and then change the source, the documentation is now outdated. If we forget to update it and check it back in, we've now got misleading documentation in our repository. So in this case, we'd want to keep a single source of the information, the source code. The same rules apply to most generated artifacts.

Pragmatically, some artifacts are difficult to regenerate. For example, you may have only a single license for a tool that generates a file needed by all the developers, or a particular artifact may take hours to create. In these cases, it makes sense to store the generated artifacts in the repository. The developer with the tool's license can create the file, or a fast machine somewhere can create the expensive artifact. These can be checked in and all other developers can then work from these generated files.

As well as all the files that go toward creating the released software, you should also store all your non-code project artifacts under version control (anything that you'll need to make sense of things later on), including the project's documentation (both internal and external). It might also include the text of significant e-mails, minutes of meetings, information you find on the web—anything that contributes to the project.

2.3 Workspaces and Manipulating Files

The repository stores all the files in our project, but that doesn't help us much if we need to add some magic new feature into our application; we need the files where *we* can get to them. This place is called our local *workspace*. The workspace is a local copy of all of the things that we need from the repository to work on our part of the project. For small to medium-sized projects, the workspace will probably simply be a copy of all the code and other artifacts in the project. For larger projects, you may arrange things so that developers can work with just a subset of the project's code, saving them time when building, and helping to isolate subsystems of the system. You might also hear the workspace called the *working directory* or the *working copy* of the code.

workspace

In order to populate our workspace initially, we need to get things out of the repository. Different version control systems have different names for this process, but the most common (and the one used by CVS) is *checking out*. When you check out from the repository, you extract local copies of files into your workspace.[1] The check out process ensures that you get up-to-date copies of the files you request, and that these files are copied into a directory structure that mirrors that of the repository.

check out

As you work on a project, you'll make changes to the project's code in your local workspace. Every now and then you'll reach a point where you'll want to save your changes back to the repository. This process is called *committing*; you're committing your changes back into the repository.

commit

Of course, all the time that you're making changes, so are other members of your team. They'll also be committing their changes to the repository. However, these changes do not affect your local workspace; it doesn't suddenly change just because someone else saved changes back into the repository. Instead, you have to instruct the version control system to *update* your local workspace. During the update, you'll receive

update

[1]Even if you do your work on the same computer that stores the repository, you'll still need to check files out before using them; the repository should be treated as a black box.

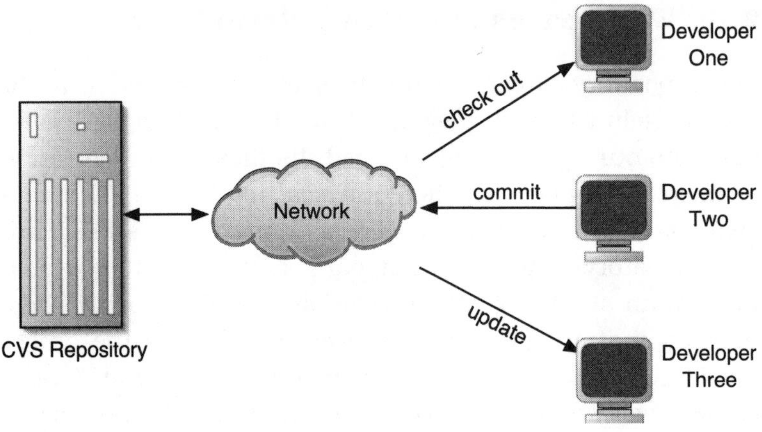

Figure 2.1: CLIENTS AND A REPOSITORY

the latest set of files from the repository. And when your colleagues do an update, they'll receive your latest changes too. (Just to confuse things, however, some folks also use the term "check out" to refer to updating, as they are checking out the latest changes. Because this is a common idiom, we'll also use this at times in this book.) These various interactions are shown in Figure 2.1.

Of course there's a potential problem here: what happens if you and a colleague both want to make changes to the same source file at the same time? It depends on the version control system you're using, but all have ways of dealing with the situation. We talk about this more in the section on page 19 on *locking options*.

2.4 Projects, Modules, and Files

So far we've talked about storing *things*, but we haven't talked about how those things are organized.

At the lowest level, most version control systems deal with individual files.[2] Each file in your project is stored by name

[2]There are some IDE-like environments that perform versioning at the method level, but they're fairly uncommon.

in the repository; if you add a file called `Panel.java` to the repository, then other members of your team can check out `Panel.java` into their own workspaces.

However, that's pretty low-level. A typical project might have hundreds or thousands of files, and a typical company might have dozens of projects. Fortunately, almost all version control systems allow you to structure the repository. At the top level, they typically divide your work into projects. With each project, they then let you work in terms of modules (and often submodules). For example, perhaps you are working on *Orinoco*, a large web-based book ordering application. All the files needed to build the application might be stored in the repository under the Orinoco project name. If you wanted to, you could check it all out onto your local disk.

The Orinoco project itself might be broken down into a number of largely independent modules. For example, there might be a team working on credit card processing and another working on order fulfillment. With any luck, the folks in the credit card subproject won't need to have all the project's source to do their job; their code should be nicely partitioned. So when they check out, they really only want to see the parts of the project that they're working on.

CVS allows the repository administrator to divide a project into *modules*. A module is a group of files (normally contained *module* in one or more file system directory trees) that can be checked out by name. Modules can be hierarchical, but they don't have to be; the same file or set of files can appear in many different modules. Modules even let you share code between projects (simply put the files to be shared into a module and let the other team reference it by name).

Modules give you many different views into your repository, allowing people in your teams to deal only with the things they need. We talk about modules in Chapter 9 on page 111.

2.5 Where Do Versions Come In?

This book is all about version control systems, but so far all we've talked about is storing and retrieving files in a repository. Where do versions come in?

version

Behind the scenes, a version control system's repository is a fairly clever beast. It doesn't just store the current copy of each of the files in its care. Instead it stores *every version* that has ever been checked in. If you check out a file, edit it, then check it back in, the repository will hold both the original version and the version that contains your changes.[3] Most systems use a simple numbering system for the versions of a file. In CVS, the first version of a file is assigned the revision number 1.1. If a changed version is checked in, that change is given the number 1.2. The next change gets 1.3, and so on. (We'll be talking about more complex numbering soon). Associated with each of these revision numbers is the date and time that the file was checked in, along with an optional comment from the developer describing the change.

This system of storing revisions is remarkably powerful. Using it, the version control system can do things such as:

- Retrieve a specific revision of a file.
- Check out all of the source code of a system as it appeared two months ago.
- Tell you what changed in a particular file between versions 1.3 and 1.5.

You can also use the revision system to undo mistakes. If you get to the end of the week and discover you've been going down a blind alley, you can back out all the changes you've made, reverting back to the code as it was on Monday morning.

There's a small wrinkle to the way revisions are numbered. Some version control systems assign a single revision number to all the files affected by a particular check in, while others give each file a unique sequence of revision numbers. CVS falls in to the latter camp. For example, we might check three files out of a repository and get the following version numbers:

```
File1.java     1.10
File2.java     1.7
File3.java     1.9
```

[3]In reality, most version control systems store the differences between versions of a file, rather than complete copies of each revision.

We edit `File1.java` and `File3.java`, but leave `File2.java` untouched. If we commit these changes back to the repository, it will increment the revision numbers on those files we changed:

```
File1.java      1.11
File2.java      1.7
File3.java      1.10
```

This means you can't use the individual file version numbers to keep track of things such as project releases (Version 1.3a of the Orinoco project, for example). Because this one point often causes grief in teams just starting to use CVS, let's repeat it. *The individual revision numbers that CVS assigns to files should not be used as external version numbers.* Instead, version control systems provide you with *tags* (or their equivalent).

2.6 Tags

All these revision numbers are great, but as people we seem to be better at remembering names such as "PreRelease2" rather than numbers like 1.47. We also have a problem when the different files that make up a particular release of our software have different revision numbers. In the previous example, we might be ready to ship the software built with `File1.java`, `File2.java`, and `File3.java`, but each file has its own revision number. So how do you tie all these different numbers together?

Tags to the rescue. Version control systems let you assign names to a group of files (or modules, or an entire project) at a particular point in time. If you assigned the tag "PreRelease2" to this group of three files, you could subsequently check them out using that same tag. You'd get revision 1.11 of `File1.java`, 1.7 of `File2.java`, and 1.10 of `File3.java`. *tag*

Tags are a great way of keeping track of significant events in the history of your project's code. We'll be using tags extensively later in this document. In fact, tags and branches (the topic of the next section) have their own chapter, starting on page 91.

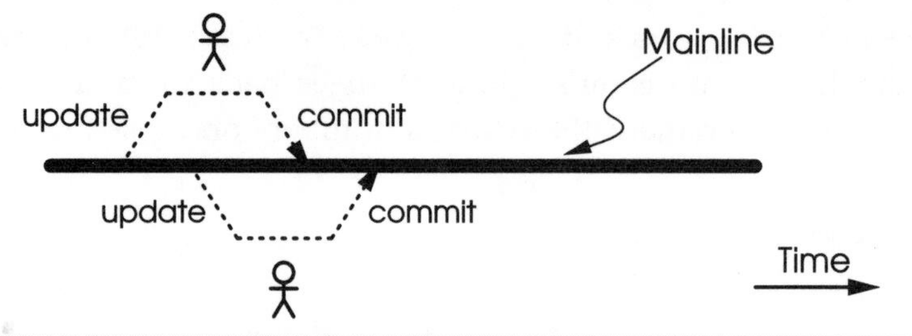

Figure 2.2: A SIMPLE MAINLINE

2.7 Branches

In the normal course of development, most folks are working on a common code base (although they'll likely be working on different parts of it). They'll be checking stuff out, making revisions, and checking the changes back in, and everyone will share this work. This river of code is often called a *mainline*. We show this in Figure 2.2. In this figure (and in the ones that follow) time flows from left to right. The thicker horizontal line represents the progression of code through time; it is the mainline of the development. Individual developers check in and check out code from this mainline into their individual workspaces.

mainline

But consider the time when a new release is about to be shipped. One small subteam of developers may be preparing the software for that release, fixing last minute bugs, working with the release engineers, and helping the QA team. During this vital period, they need stability; it would set back their efforts if other developers were also editing the code, adding features intended for the next release.

One option is to freeze new development while the release is being generated, but this means that the rest of the team is effectively sitting idle.

Another option would be to copy the source software out onto a spare machine and then have the release team just use this machine. But if we do that, what happens to the changes that they make after the copy? How do we keep track of them? If they find bugs in the release code that are also in the mainline, how can we efficiently and reliably merge these fixes back in? And once they've released the software, how do we fix bugs that customers report; how can we guarantee to find the source code in the same state as when we shipped the release?

A far better option is to use the branching capabilities built into version control systems.

Branching is a bit like the hackneyed device in science fiction stories where some event causes time to split. From that point forward there are two parallel futures. Some other event occurs, and one of these futures splits too. Soon you're dealing with a whole bunch of alternative universes (a great device for resolving the story when you run out of plot ideas).

branch

Branching in a version control system also allows you to create multiple parallel futures, but rather than being populated by aliens and space cowboys, they contain source code and version information.

Take the case of the team about to release a new version of the product. So far, all the team has been working in the *mainline*, the common thread of code shown in Figure 2.2 on the preceding page. But the release subteam wants to isolate themselves from this mainline. To do this, they create a branch in the repository. From now until their work is done, the release subteam will check out from and check in to this branch. Even after the application is released, this branch will stay active; if customers report bugs, the team will fix them in this release branch. This situation is shown in Figure 2.3 on the following page.

A branch is almost like having a totally separate repository: people using that branch see the source code it contains and operate independently of people working on other branches or the mainline. Each branch has its own history and tracks revisions people make independently (although obviously if you look back past the point where the branch was made you'll see that the branch and the mainline become one).

This is exactly what you want when you're creating releases. The team working on the release will have a stable code base to polish up and ship. In the meantime, the main group of developers can continue making changes to the main line of

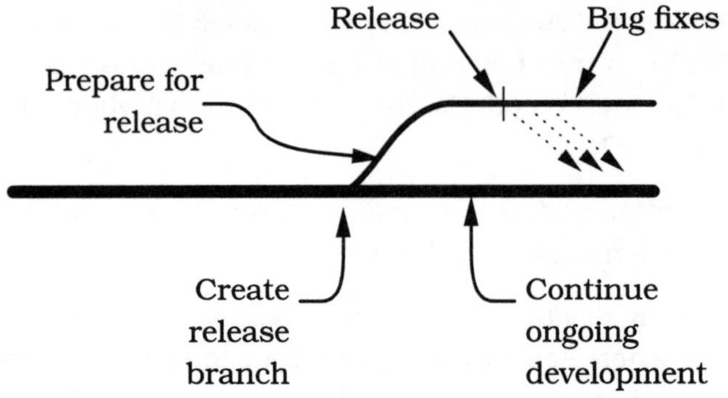

Figure 2.3: MAINLINE WITH A RELEASE BRANCH

code; there's no need for a code freeze while the release takes place. And when customers report problems in the release, the team will have access to the code in the release branch so they can fix the bugs and ship updated releases without including any of the newly developed code in the mainline.

Branches are identified by tags, and file revision numbers within a branch have extra levels in their numbers. So if `File1.java` is at revision 1.14 and you create a branch, you'll find that in the branch it may have a revision number of 1.14.2.1, while in the mainline it's still 1.14. Edit it in the mainline and you'll get revision 1.15; edit in the branch and the revision number will be 1.14.2.2.

You can create branches off of other branches, but typically you won't want to; we've come across many developers who have been put off branching for life because of some bad experiences with overly complicated branching in a project. In this book we'll describe a simple scheme that does everything you'll need but that avoids unnecessary complexity.

2.8 Merging

Back to the science fiction story with the multiple alternate futures. In order to spice up the plot, writers often allow their characters to travel between these different universes using wormholes, polyphase deconfabulating oscillotrons, or just a good strong cup of piping hot tea.

You can also travel between alternate futures in a version control system (the cup of tea is optional). Although each checked out version comes from a particular branch, and gets checked back in to that branch, it's easy to have multiple branches checked out on a single developer's machine (in different directories or folders on the hard drive, of course). That way a developer can be working on both the mainline and on (say) bug fixes in a release branch at the same time.

Even better, version control systems support merging. Say you fix a bug in the release branch and realize that the same bug will be present in the mainline code. You can tell the version control system to work out the changes you made to the source while you fixed the bug, and then to apply those changes to the code in the mainline. This largely eliminates the need to cut and paste changes back and forth between different versions of a system. We'll have a lot to say about merging later on. *merge*

2.9 Locking Options

Imagine two developers, Fred and Wilma, working on the same project. Each has checked out the project's files onto their respective local hard drives, and each wants to edit their local copy of `File1.java`. What happens when they come to check that file back in?

A bad scenario would be for the version control system to accept Fred's changes, and then accept Wilma's version of the same file. As Wilma's copy won't have Fred's changes in it, storing Wilma's copy in the repository will effectively forget all Fred's hard work.

To stop this happening, version control systems implement some form of conflict resolution system (probably a good thing in the case of Fred and Wilma). There are two common versions of conflict resolution.

The first is called *strict locking*. In a strict locking version control system, all files that are checked out are initially flagged as being "read only." You can look at them, and you can use them to build your application, but you can't edit or change *strict locking* them. To do that, you have to ask the repository's permission: "please can I edit File1.java?" If no one else is editing that same file, then the repository gives you permission and changes the permissions of your local copy of the file to be "read/write." You can then edit. If anyone else asks to edit that same file while you have it flagged, they'll be refused. After you've finished your changes and checked the file back in, your local copy reverts back to being read only, and it becomes available for other folks to edit.

optimistic locking

The second form of conflict resolution is often called *optimistic locking,* although it really is no locking at all. Here, every developer gets to edit any checked out file: the files are checked out in a read/write state. However, the repository will not allow you to check in a file that has been updated in the repository since you last checked it out. Instead, it asks you to update your local copy of the file to include the latest repository changes before checking in. This is where the cleverness lies. Instead of simply overwriting all your hard work with the latest repository version of the file, the version control system attempts to merge the repository changes with your changes. For example, let's look at `File1.java`:

```
Line 1  public class File1 {
-         public String getName() {
-           return "Wibble";
-         }
5         public int getSize() {
-           return 42;
-         }
-       }
```

Wilma and Fred both check this file out. Fred changes line 3:

```
return "WIBBLE";
```

He then checks the file back in. This means that Wilma's copy of the file is out of date. Not knowing this, Wilma changes line 6, so it returns 99 instead of 42. When she goes to check the file in, she's told that her copy is out of date; she needs to merge in the repository changes. This corresponds to the star marked **CONFLICT** in Figure 2.4 on the next page.

When Wilma merges the changes into her file, the version control system is clever enough to spot that Fred's changes do not overlap hers, so it simply updates her local copy with a new

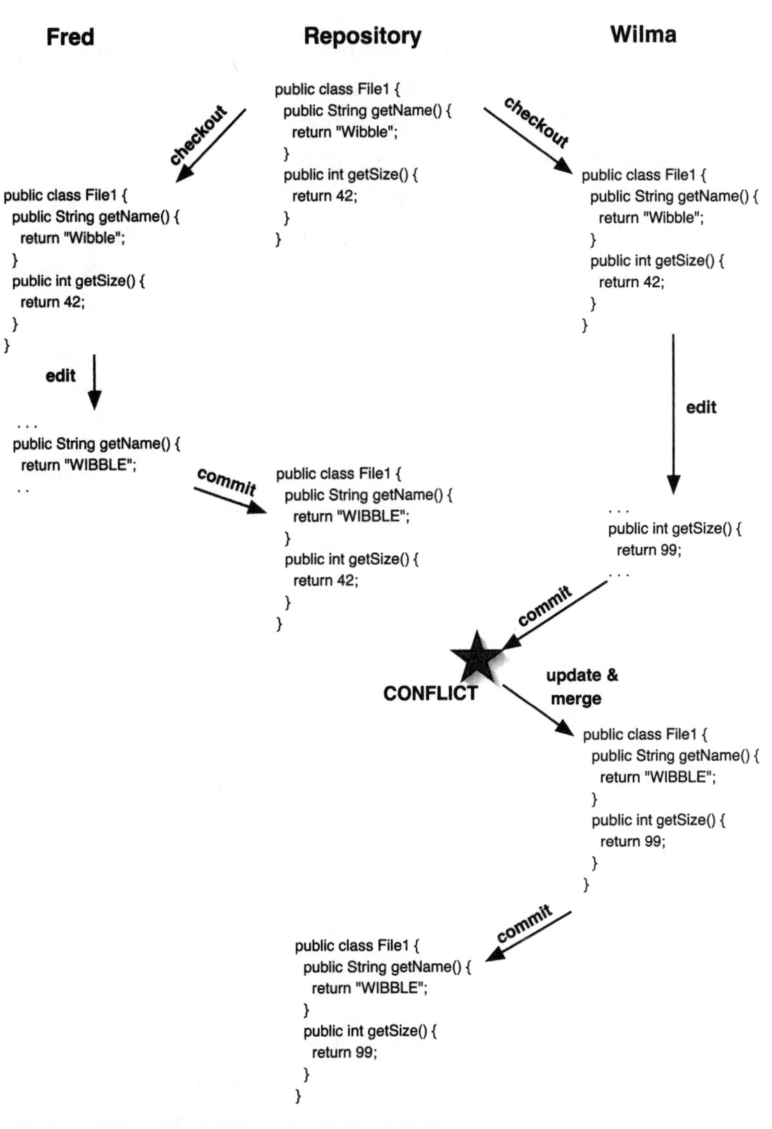

Figure 2.4: FRED AND WILMA MAKE CHANGES TO THE SAME FILE, BUT THE CONFLICT IS HANDLED BY A MERGE.

line 3, leaving her changes still in her file. When she checks in, she'll be storing back her changes and leaving Fred's intact.

What happens if Fred and Wilma both updated line 3, but made different changes to it? Assuming Fred checks in first, his changes will be accepted. When Wilma goes to check in, she'll again be told that her copy is out of date. This time, though, when she goes to merge in the repository version the system will notice that she's made a change to a line that has also been changed in the repository. There's a conflict. In this case, Wilma will see some warning messages, and the conflict will be marked up in her copy of the source file. She'll have to resolve it manually (probably by talking with Fred to find out why they were both working on the same line of code).

Given this description you might think that optimistic locking is a somewhat reckless way of developing systems: multiple people editing the same files at the same time. Often people who haven't tried it reason that it can't work, and insist on working only with version control systems that implement strict locking.

In reality, though, strict locking turns out to be a lot of extra hassle with no particular payback. If you try an optimistic locking system (such as CVS) you'll be surprised at just how rarely conflicts arise. It turns out that in practice the normal ways of dividing up work on a team mean that people work on different areas of the code; they don't bump in to each other that often. And when they *do* need to edit the same file, they're often working on different parts of it. In a strict locking system, one would have to wait for the other to finish and check in before proceeding. In an optimistic locking system, both can proceed. We've tried both kinds of locking over the years, and our strong recommendation is that the vast majority of teams should use a version control system with optimistic locking.

2.10 Configuration Management (CM)

Sometimes you'll hear folks talking about Configuration Management or Software Configuration Management systems (often abbreviated as CM or SCM). At first sight they seem to be talking about version control. And that's largely true; the practices of CM rely very heavily on having good version control in place. But version control is just one tool used by configuration management.

CM is a set of project management practices that enables you to accurately and reproducibly deliver software. It uses version control to achieve its technical goals, but also uses a lot of human controls and cross checks to make sure that things are not forgotten. You can think of configuration management as a way of identifying the things that get delivered, and version control as a means of recording that identification. CM is a large (and to some extent ill-defined) topic, and we won't be covering it more in this book.

For now, though, let's concentrate on how to use version control systems to get our jobs done. The next chapter is a gentle introduction to a particular version control system, CVS.

Chapter 3

Getting Started

Before committing your next multi-million dollar project to CVS, it's probably a good idea to get some experience with the system first. In this chapter we'll work with a live CVS repository as we develop and maintain a trivial project.

As is often the case, the first steps with CVS are often the most difficult.

- You may have to install the CVS software on your computer.
- Before you can use a repository to check in a project, the repository has to be set up, and you must have access to it.

You also have a number of choices when it comes to interacting with this repository. You can use the traditional CVS command-line tools, you can use a GUI front-end, and you can use facilities built into your IDE.

Finally, there are some differences depending on the operating system you use. We'll highlight these as we go along.

We'll take all these things one step at a time.

3.1 Installing CVS

Obviously, you need to install the CVS software before you can run it. The same software both manages the repository

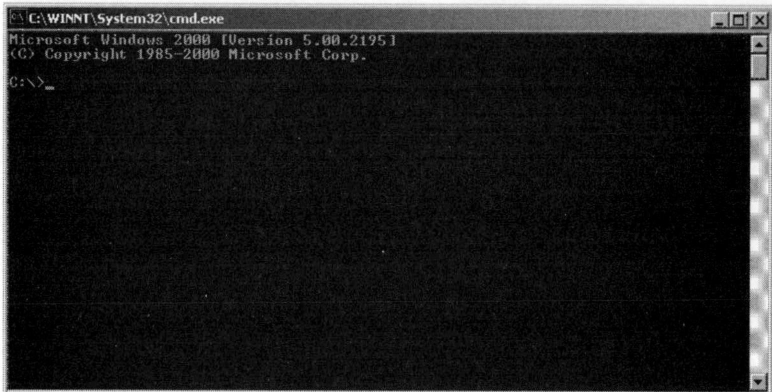

Figure 3.1: WINDOWS COMMAND WINDOW

and gives you the command-line tools you need to access that repository.

Our first step is to determine if CVS is already installed on your computer. The easiest way to do this is from the command line. If you're familiar with the command line, you can skip the next section.

The Command Line

The command line is a low-level facility that lets you run commands directly on your computer. The command line is a powerful tool, but it can also be fairly cryptic: you're working down in the engine room when you're issuing commands.

On Windows boxes, you can get to a command line window by using [Start]/[Run], and typing `cmd` as the name of the program to run (on some older Windows versions you might have to type `command` instead). You should see a window that looks like Figure 3.1.

On Unix boxes, you may be working at the command line already. If instead you use a desktop environment such as Gnome or KDE, look for the `terminal`, `konsole`, or `xterm` application and run it. You should see a window like that in

Figure 3.2: UNIX COMMAND WINDOW

Figure 3.3: WINDOW AFTER EXECUTING "ECHO HELLO"

Figure 3.2. (If you're using Mac OS X, your shell application is hidden in /Applications/Utilities/Terminal.)

You use the command line window to enter commands and view their output; no GUI front ends here. For example, in the command line window you just created, enter the following

Joe Asks...

Shells, Prompts, Command Windows??

Terminology can get confusing when we're dealing with command-lines, so let's clear things up a bit.

A command processor, also called a shell, is a program that accepts a command and executes it. The command can have parameters, and the command processor often has additional capabilities (such as redirecting the application's output to a file). Under Windows, `cmd` and `command` are common command processors (which you use depends on which version of Windows you use). On Unix boxes, there's a great choice of shells, from the original `sh`, through `csh`, `bash`, `tcsh`, `zsh`, and so on.

Back before we had GUI systems, the command processor or shell was how you interacted with your computer. When you booted up DOS, you got the DOS prompt, and you were talking with the `command` application; your computer monitor was effectively a dumb terminal.

Now that we have fancy front ends, we need a place to run these command processors, so folks have written terminal applications that run in windows. When one of these terminal applications is running a command processor or a shell, you can type in commands at the prompt and have them execute. Sometimes we'll call these windows executing a command processor a *command window*.

command and hit the Enter key (sometimes labeled Return).

```
echo Hello
```

You should see the text "Hello" echoed back at you, and just below it a new prompt where you can enter another command. An example is shown in Figure 3.3 on the preceding page.

Prompts

One of the joys of the command window is that you can customize the prompt that the shell uses to tell you it's ready for input. You can include the time, the current directory, your user name, and all sorts of other essential information in the prompt field. Unfortunately, this flexibility can also lead to confusion: looking back at the previous screenshots you can see that the Windows prompt looks totally different from the Unix prompt.

In this book, we'll try to simplify things by standardizing on a generic prompt in our examples. We'll show the name of the current directory followed by a greater-than sign (">"). For example, we might give an example of a command as follows:

```
work> cvs update
```

This means that we're in a directory called "work" and we issued the command `cvs update`. It should be simple to map this "logical" prompt to the prompt you actually see in your operating system's command window.

The commands in this book are not Windows or Unix specific: they should work on both systems. The only differences are in the names of files; Windows uses drive letters and backward slashes between the components of file names, and Unix uses forward slashes. Use appropriate file names for your environment, and things should work out fine.

Is CVS Installed?

Bring up a command window on your computer and enter the command "`cvs -v`" (followed by the Return key, but you knew that...). If CVS is correctly installed on your box you'll see something similar to Figure 3.4 on the next page, and you can skip ahead to the next section.

-v ⇒ *Version*

If CVS isn't installed on your computer, you'll need to install it. This isn't tricky, but it depends on your operating system, and potentially on your company's policies (if you're running this exercise on a corporate computer). So rather than rein-

```
sh <2>
dave$ cvs -v

Concurrent Versions System (CVS) 1.11 (client/server)

Copyright (c) 1989-2000 Brian Berliner, david d 'zoo' zuhn,
                        Jeff Polk, and other authors

CVS may be copied only under the terms of the GNU General Public License,
a copy of which can be found with the CVS distribution kit.

Specify the --help option for further information about CVS
dave$ 
```

Figure 3.4: DETERMINING THE CVS VERSION

vent the wheel here, we'll refer you over to the home of CVS,[1] where you'll find all the materials you'll need to download and install your own copy of CVS. If you're a Windows user, you'll find a pre-built binary distribution in the the `cvshome` downloads section. If you're a Unix user, you can either build from the source on their site, or (if you'd prefer), you can find a prepackaged binary version from your distribution's vendor. (For example, if you're running a Redhat system, there are RPMs that will install CVS on your system). Whichever system you're installing for, remember to make sure that the various CVS programs are in your PATH so that you can use them from the command line. We'll see you after you've finished. . . .

3.2 Creating a Repository

CVS needs a repository to run. In this step we'll create one, just for ourselves, to play with.

Now you may already have access to a CVS repository; perhaps your company has one set up. For now we'll ignore it, and run with our own. This gives us the ability to play freely without worrying about messing things up. You might want to leave this repository lying around for a while, too. Sometimes

[1] `http://www.cvshome.org`

when you need to experiment to see how best to do things, it's useful to have a sandbox to play safely in.

You have a single decision to make before creating the repository: where to put it on your hard drive. The CVS repository consists of a hierarchy of files and directories in the regular filesystem on your computer. All you have to do is tell CVS where the top of this hierarchy is. In the examples that follow, we assume that you use the directory `sandbox` for your repository. Windows users can reference this directory as `C:\sandbox`, while Unix users can put it in their home directory using `~/sandbox`.

The simplest way to create a repository is using `cvs init` command from the command line.

```
Unix:     cvs -d ~/sandbox init
Windows:  cvs -d C:\sandbox init
```

The `-d` parameter tells CVS where the repository is (it's a little known fact that "repository" starts with a silent and invisible letter "d"). You can think of the `-d` option as defining the destination of CVS commands.

`-d` ⇒ *Destination*

If you want, you can list the contents of the repository directory you just created: you should find that it contains a single subdirectory, `CVSROOT`, which holds some administrative files. Congratulations; you're now a CVS administrator!

We'll now go on to add a project to this repository. However, remember that you never create files in this repository directly: you can only manipulate it using CVS commands.

3.3 CVS Commands

Up until now we've been using the command line to interact with CVS. If you prefer something prettier, various developers have written GUI front ends to CVS; rather than work at the command-line level, you can instead point and click to achieve the same thing. Some developers like this style of interface, others prefer the underlying commands.

Among the more popular front ends are the open source products WinCvs[2] and Tortoise CVS.[3] The latter product is particularly interesting, as it adds CVS client support to the Window's Explorer. There is also mention on the Tortoise CVS site of a project[4] to add CVS support to Visual Studio, although this project is still in beta status as of September, 2003.

If you normally use an IDE for development, you should also look to see if that IDE supports CVS directly. Many (including the popular open source IDE Eclipse) do, and this can be a real time saver. Check your IDE's documentation for details.

Having talked about all these fancy front ends, it's important to remember that knowing the underlying command line interface is important; when you come to automating some of your development tasks, that automation will need to interact with the repository, and it will do that using the command line interface. For that reason (and because showing every possible GUI-based interface would be impossible), in the descriptions that follow we'll show the command line interface to CVS. However, the terms we use should map directly onto the terminology of any GUI interface you use.

3.4 Creating a Simple Project

In this section we'll start to populate our repository with a new project (every good project has a name, so we'll call this project *Sesame*). We'll do this by creating a couple of files, and then importing them into a `sesame` project in our repository. (The project name is officially Sesame, with an uppercase "S," but we'll use lowercase for the project name in the repository.)

So, let's assume that we're just starting work on the Sesame project. We don't yet have a project in the repository, because we don't yet have anything to put in it. Let's fix that. Create a temporary directory on your computer (we'll call ours `tmpdir`). Then, using your favorite editor or IDE, create two files in the this directory: `Color.txt` and `Number.txt`.

---

[2] `http://www.wincvs.org`

[3] `http://www.tortoisecvs.org`

[4] `http://sourceforge.net/projects/cvssccplugin/`

File `Color.txt`:

```
black
brown
red
orange
yellow
green
```

File `Number.txt`:

```
zero
one
two
three
four
```

Hmm, I hear folks saying, these sure don't look like source programs. But remember, we use our repository to hold *all* the stuff we need to build our project. Perhaps we're working on a children's education program, and these files contain data for a particular game. (Well, it *could* happen...)

We now need to tell CVS that these files should be imported in to a new project in the repository. To do this, we'll use the `cvs import` command. It's unfortunate that we're having to use `import` so soon in the book, as it has the most mandatory parameters of any CVS command. For now, we won't go into too much detail; we cover `cvs import` in more detail on page 104.

To import the two files we just created from the command line, go to the temporary directory that contains them. If you're using a Windows box, issue the following command.

```
tmpdir>  cvs -d C:\sandbox import -m "" sesame sesame initial
N sesame/Color.txt
N sesame/Number.txt
No conflicts created by this import
```

If instead you're on a Unix platform, do:

```
tmpdir>  cvs -d ~/sandbox import -m "" sesame sesame initial
N sesame/Color.txt
N sesame/Number.txt
No conflicts created by this import
```

The `-d` parameter does the same thing here that it did on the `cvs init` command—it tells CVS where to find the repository. The `import` keyword tells CVS that we want to import a project. The `-m` and the empty string that follow it lets you

-m ⇒ *Message*

associate a log message with this import. There are circumstances where this is useful (particularly when dealing with third-party code), but for now an empty log message is fine.

The next parameter, `sesame`, is the name to give the project in the repository. This is how you'll refer to it in future, so choose wisely.

The last two parameters are tags; we won't worry about them for now. If you want to import your own code, using the project name for the first tag and "initial" for the second will work just fine.

Notice that as CVS performs the import, it logs what it is doing. In this case it shows the names of our two files with an "N" in front of them. This means that they are new, and that they have been added to the repository.

So, now we've got these files safely tucked away in the repository. If we are brave (or foolish), we can go ahead and delete the copies in our temporary directory. However, the prudent (and pragmatic) developer would probably want to verify that they are indeed correctly stored in the repository before deleting them. And the easiest way to do that is to get CVS to check the files in the Sesame project out into your local work area. Once we've confirmed that everything is there, and that it looks correct, we can delete our originals. The next section shows how this is done.

3.5 Starting to Work With a Project

It doesn't matter whether you're starting work with a new project (such as project Sesame, which we just created), or if you're joining a project that's been running for months and has thousands of source files. What you do to start working with the project's files is the same:

1. Decide where to put the working copies of the files on your local machine.
2. Check the project out of the repository into that location.

The first decision is normally fairly simple. We tend to have a single directory on our boxes called "`work`." We then check all

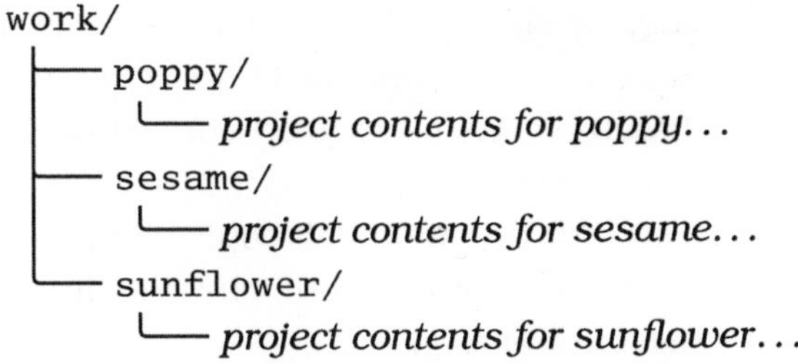

Figure 3.5: A CHECKED-OUT TREE

projects somewhere under this directory. For simple projects, we tend to check out directly under work/. For more complex ones, we need to create a local workspace. For now, let's assume we are working with simple projects. If we have checked out three separate projects called poppy, sesame, and sunflower, we'd end up with directories that looked something like Figure 3.5.

So, if you haven't already got one, let's start off by creating a work directory, either from the command line or using your File Manager.

```
Unix:     mkdir ~/work
Windows:  mkdir \work
```

Now we'll check the project out into this directory. The -d option tells CVS where to find the repository, the co stands for *check out*, and the sesame is the name of the project.

```
Unix:     cd ~/work
          cvs -d ~/sandbox co sesame
Windows:  cd \work
          cvs -d C:\sandbox co sesame
```

You should see some output that looks something like:

```
work> cvs -d ~/sandbox co sesame
cvs checkout: Updating sesame
U sesame/Color.txt
U sesame/Number.txt
```

You now have a local copy of the Sesame project containing the two files that we initially imported. From now on, we'll be working with these copies of the files, because these are the ones that are being managed by CVS. After checking that they look correct, we can go ahead and delete the original copies in our temporary directory. We've handed control of these files over to our version control system, and it's just too confusing to have the original and the managed copies lying around on our machine. We'll make `sesame` our current directory and work with the checked-out files.

3.6 Making Changes

Despite all our hard work, our customer comes back complaining; it appears we're several colors short of a full palette. So, fire up your favorite editor and add the four lines to the end of the file:

File `Color.txt`:

```
black
brown
red
orange
yellow
green
blue     ┐
purple   │ add these lines
gray     │
white    ┘
```

After saving these changes to disk, let's see what CVS now thinks about the state of our project. We can use the `cvs status` command to give us the status of one or more files.

```
work/sesame>  cvs status Color.txt
===================================================================
File: Color.txt             Status: Locally Modified

   Working revision:     1.1.1.1 Fri Jan  2 16:45:50 2004
   Repository revision: 1.1.1.1 /Users/.../sesame/Color.txt,v
   Sticky Tag:           (none)
   Sticky Date:          (none)
   Sticky Options:       (none)
```

The important line here is the status: CVS recognizes that this file has been modified locally (and that these changes have not yet been saved in the repository).

If we do all our work in small increments, it's easy to remember what changes we made to individual files. However, if we've forgotten why a file has been modified (or if we just want to double-check), we can use the `cvs diff` command to show us the changes between the repository version of the file and our local copy:

```
work/sesame>  cvs diff Color.txt
Index: Color.txt
===================================================
RCS file: /Users/dave/sandbox/sesame/Color.txt,v
retrieving revision 1.1.1.1
diff -r1.1.1.1 Color.txt
6a7,10
> blue
> purple
> gray
> white
```

The output contains a bunch of information. The first line tells us the name of the file being examined. This has a couple of uses. First, if we're examining a bunch of files with one command, it helps us identify where we are. It is also used when generating patches (but that's not something we'll be looking at for a while yet).

The three lines after the row of equals signs tell us the name and revision number of the repository file, along with the low-level command that's being used to generate the diff.

The somewhat cryptic "`6a7,10`" tells us that after line 6 we've added new lines 7 through 10. Following this, the logging lines starting with ">" show the actual lines that were added.

The command-line CVS has a feature which displays the local and repository versions of a file side-by-side:

```
work/sesame>  cvs diff --side-by-side Color.txt
Index: Color.txt
===================================================
RCS file: /Users/dave/sandbox/sesame/Color.txt,v
retrieving revision 1.1.1.1
diff --side-by-side -r1.1.1.1 Color.txt
black                                        black
brown                                        brown
red                                          red
orange                                       orange
yellow                                       yellow
green                                        green
                                           > blue
                                           > purple
                                           > gray
                                           > white
```

This is an area where the GUI front-ends to CVS have a distinct advantage: if you use such a tool you'll probably find that you'll be able to generate nice color-coded displays of file differences.

3.7 Updating the Repository

Having made our changes (and of course having run the unit tests), we're ready to save our latest version in the repository. On a single-person project such as Sesame, this is really very simple—you use the `cvs commit` command.

```
work/sesame>  cvs commit -m "Client wants 4 more colors"
cvs commit: Examining .
Checking in Color.txt;
/Users/dave/sandbox/sesame/Color.txt,v  <--  Color.txt
new revision: 1.2; previous revision: 1.1
done
```

The `commit` function is used to save any changes we've made back in to the repository. The `-m` option is used to attach a meaningful message to the changes. If you don't specify the `-m` option, CVS will pop open an editor window and ask you to enter one; this can be somewhat disconcerting the first time it happens.

Even though we asked CVS to commit all files in the Sesame project, it's clever enough to know that `Number.txt` has not changed, so only `Color.txt` gets updated to a new revision (1.2 in this case).

Following the commit, use the status function to show us that the repository has indeed been updated:

```
work/sesame>  cvs status Color.txt
===================================================================
File: Color.txt          Status: Up-to-date

   Working revision:     1.2 Thu Apr 17 17:26:17 2003
   Repository revision: 1.2 /Users/.../sesame/Color.txt,v
   Sticky Tag:           (none)
   Sticky Date:          (none)
   Sticky Options:       (none)
```

We can also look at the history of the file (CVS calls this the file's *log*).

```
work/sesame>  cvs log Color.txt

RCS file: /Users/dave/sandbox/sesame/Color.txt,v
Working file: Color.txt
head: 1.2
branch:
locks: strict
access list:
symbolic names:
keyword substitution: kv
total revisions: 2;     selected revisions: 2
description:
----------------------------
revision 1.2
```

```
date: 2003/04/17 18:24:56; author: dave; state: Exp; lines: +4 -0
Client wants 4 more colors
----------------------------
revision 1.1
date: 2003/04/17 17:11:36;  author: dave;  state: Exp;
=============================================================
```

3.8 When Worlds Collide

Everyone gets nervous when they first hear that CVS doesn't lock files for editing. They wonder, "What happens if two people edit the same file at the same time?" In this section we'll find out (and hopefully in the process put any worries you may have to rest). To do this, we'll need another user (so that we can have multiple people editing a file at the same time). Unfortunately, our supplier of do-it-yourself human cloning kits is on the run, so we'll have to make do with simulating the other you.

When it comes to handling conflicts, CVS doesn't really know about users. Instead, it cares about making sure that files in different workspaces are consistent. This means that we can simulate our second user simply by checking out a new copy of our project; we just need to put it in a different place than the first copy. When we first checked out our project, CVS put it in a directory called `sesame`, which is the project name. To check it out again, we'll need to override that default behavior. There is only one rule; do not check out the second copy of the project inside the current `sesame` project directory. Instead, check it out in to a directory parallel to the one we've been working in. Let's call that directory `aladdin`. To do this, we use a second `-d` option, specifying the new directory name.

`-d` ⇒ *Target Directory*

Unix:
```
cd ~/work
cvs -d ~/sandbox co -d aladdin sesame
```
Windows:
```
cd \work
cvs -d C:\sandbox co -d aladdin sesame
```

CVS will generate output that is something like the following.

```
cvs checkout: Updating aladdin
U aladdin/Color.txt
U aladdin/Number.txt
```

We've checked out the project we've been working on all along (Sesame) from the same `sandbox` repository. But we tell CVS to store the files in a new directory, called `aladdin`. Because we checked in the files from our original directory, we now have two copies of the project on our hard drive, one in `sesame`, the other in `aladdin`. Right now the two sets of files are identical (skeptical readers, feel free to check). Remember that two different directories are our simulation of having two people working on our project, each with their own checked-out copy of the files.

Let's first do a quick sanity check. We'll alter a file in one directory, check it in, then ask CVS to update our local copy in the other directory.

First, edit the file `Number.txt` in the `sesame` directory, adding two new lines (*five* and *six*):

File `Number.txt`:

```
zero
one
two
three
four
five
six
```

Now check this file back in to the repository:

```
work/sesame>  cvs commit -m "Customer needed more numbers"
cvs commit: Examining .
Checking in Number.txt;
/Users/dave/sandbox/sesame/Number.txt,v  <--  Number.txt
new revision: 1.2; previous revision: 1.1
done
```

Now for the first moment of truth. Over in the `aladdin` directory, its version of `Number.txt` is now out of date (because the repository now holds a more recent version). Let's pop over there and check.

```
work/sesame>  cd ../aladdin
work/aladdin>  cvs status Number.txt
=====================================================
File: Number.txt          Status: Needs Patch
   Working revision:      1.1 Thu Apr 17 17:11:36 2003
   Repository revision: 1.2 /Users/.../sesame/Number.txt,v
   Sticky Tag:            (none)
   Sticky Date:           (none)
   Sticky Options:        (none)
```

The *status* line tells us that our copy of the file needs patching (updating) to bring it up to date. Before we do this, we might ask CVS to tell us what's different between our version of the file and the version currently in the repository (as there are times when you might want to defer an update if it affects stuff you're currently working on). Again, we use the `cvs diff` command.

```
work/aladdin> cvs diff -rHEAD Number.txt
Index: Number.txt
===================================================================
RCS file: /Users/dave/sandbox/sesame/Number.txt,v
retrieving revision 1.2
retrieving revision 1.1
diff -r1.2 -r1.1
6,7d5
< five
< six
```

The `-rHEAD` option tells CVS that we want to compare our local copy of `Number.txt` against whatever revision is the most recent in the repository (the head of the branch). After another one of those cryptic `6,7d5` lines, we see that two new lines have been added (which shouldn't be a surprise). If we hadn't specified the `-r` flag, CVS would compare our local copy of `Number.txt` against the repository version that was checked out to produce it (1.1 in this case). As we haven't altered the file in our Aladdin persona, this would show no changes.

`-r` ⇒ *Revision*

We can update our copy in the `aladdin` directory to merge in the changes we made over in `sesame`.

```
work/aladdin> cvs update
cvs update: Updating .
U Number.txt
```

The tracing shows that CVS has Updated the `Number.txt` file locally. If we look at it, we'll see that we now have the two extra lines.

3.9 Conflict Resolution

So, what happens if two people edit the same file at the same time? It turns out that there are two scenarios. The first is when the changes don't overlap. Simulating this takes a little effort, so hang in there.

First, edit the copy of `Number.txt` in the `sesame` directory. Make the first line upper case.

File `Number.txt (in sesame)`:

```
ZERO
one
two
three
four
five
six
```

Now edit the version of `Number.txt` over in `aladdin`. This time make the last line upper case.

File `Number.txt (in aladdin)`:

```
zero
one
two
three
four
five
SIX
```

What we've just done is simulate two developers each making local changes to the same file. Right now, these changes are independent, because the repository knows about neither. Let's change that. A coin toss told us that Aladdin checked in his version of the changed file first.

```
work/aladdin> cvs commit -m "Make 'six' important"
cvs commit: Examining .
Checking in Number.txt;
/Users/dave/sandbox/sesame/Number.txt,v  <--  Number.txt
new revision: 1.3; previous revision: 1.2
done
```

A short time later, the `sesame` developer checks in too. (Remember, this version of the file has the first line in upper case.)

```
work/sesame> cvs commit -m "Zero needs emphasizing"
cvs commit: Examining .
cvs commit: Up-to-date check failed for 'Number.txt'
cvs [commit aborted]: correct above errors first!
```

Uh oh! CVS is using words such as "errors," and even ends the message with an exclamation mark. We're doomed.

Or not. Let's try doing what it (indirectly) suggests and bring our local version of the file up to date with the repository. Remember that our file has an upper case "zero," while the repository version has an upper case "six."

```
work/sesame>  cvs update
cvs update: Updating .
RCS file: /Users/dave/sandbox/sesame/Number.txt,v
retrieving revision 1.2
retrieving revision 1.3
Merging differences between 1.2 and 1.3 into Number.txt
M Number.txt
```

Notice the additional messages. CVS tells us that it isn't simply updating our local file; instead it's merging our changes with the repository version. Let's look at our local version:

File `Number.txt`:

```
ZERO
one
two
three
four
five
SIX
```

Magic! Our version now contains *both* our changes and the Aladdin changes. We both edited a file at the same time, and CVS worked it out.

Before we get too smug, though, remember that our local change (the ZERO) hasn't yet been stored in the repository. We ask CVS to commit our change and it succeeds, because our local version contains the latest repository revisions.

```
work/sesame>  cvs commit -m "Zero needs emphasizing"
cvs commit: Examining .
Checking in Number.txt;
/Users/dave/sandbox/sesame/Number.txt,v  <--  Number.txt
new revision: 1.4; previous revision: 1.3
done
```

The next time Aladdin updates, he'll get our changes too.

```
work/sesame>  cd ../aladdin
work/aladdin>  cvs update
cvs update: Updating .
U Number.txt
```

Butting Heads—When Changes Clash

In the previous example, the changes made by the two (virtual) developers didn't overlap. What happens if two developers edit the same lines in the same file at the same time? Let's find out.

Go into the `sesame` directory and change the second line in `Number.txt` from "one" to "ichi". Don't check this change in. Now go across to the `aladdin` directory and change the same line from "one" to "uno". Let's assume that once again Aladdin gets to check in his changes first.

```
work/aladdin>  cvs commit -m "User likes Italian one"
cvs commit: Examining .
Checking in Number.txt;
/Users/dave/sandbox/sesame/Number.txt,v  <--  Number.txt
new revision: 1.5; previous revision: 1.4
done
```

Now let's go back to the `sesame` directory. Remembering that we're supposed to be simulating two separate users, we pretend we don't know about the changes made by Aladdin, and so try to check in our changes.

```
work/sesame>  cvs commit -m "One should be Japanese"
cvs commit: Examining .
cvs commit: Up-to-date check failed for 'Number.txt'
cvs [commit aborted]: correct above errors first!
```

We've seen this message before: we need to update to get the repository changes.

```
work/sesame>  cvs update
cvs update: Updating .
RCS file: /Users/dave/sandbox/sesame/Number.txt,v
retrieving revision 1.4
retrieving revision 1.5
Merging differences between 1.4 and 1.5 into Number.txt
rcsmerge: warning: conflicts during merge
cvs update: conflicts found in Number.txt
C Number.txt
```

Now this looks scary: CVS is telling us that there were conflicts found while merging the repository revision in to our local changes. Have we lost all our hard work? No.

When conflicts happen, it's mostly because two developers had some kind of misunderstanding. In this case, one developer wanted to change the line to Italian, while the other wanted Japanese. If you think about this for a while, it becomes apparent that what we have here is a breakdown in communication; there's a problem in the team (or at least in the team's process). Whatever the cause, we're left wondering, "what should the line really be?" CVS doesn't have a hotline to the customer, so it can't solve the problem. Instead, it adds special annotations to the file to show what the conflict is. In this case if we look at the file `Number.txt`, we'll see it now looks like:

File `Number.txt`:

```
ZERO
<<<<<<< Number.txt
ichi
=======
uno
>>>>>>> 1.5
two
three
four
five
SIX
```

The lines with the <<<<<< and >>>>>>> show where the conflict occurred. Between them we can see both our change *and* the conflicting change in the repository. Time to do some detective work. The first thing we need to do is to find out who made the change in the repository. The `cvs log` command displays the history of one or more files, so it'll help us find out what happened here.

```
work/sesame>  cvs log -r1.5 Number.txt
RCS file: /Users/dave/sandbox/sesame/Number.txt,v
Working file: Number.txt
head: 1.5
branch:
locks: strict
access list:
symbolic names:
keyword substitution: kv
total revisions: 5;     selected revisions: 1
description:
----------------------------
revision 1.5
date: 2003/04/22 18:22:07;  author: dave;  state: Exp;  lines: +1 -1
User likes Italian one
=============================================
```

Looking at the last couple of lines, we can see the name of the author of the change, along with their check-in comment. We wander over and ask him about the change. A quick call to the customer resolves the problem: the customer wanted the word "one" in Japanese, and "two" in Italian. Aladdin must have misheard. Armed with this new information, we can now resolve the conflict. Edit `Number.txt` in the `sesame` directory, remove CVS's conflict markers, and make the changes requested by the customer.

File Number.txt (sesame):

```
ZERO
ichi
due
three
four
five
SIX
```

Having removed the conflict markers, we can now commit this file.

```
work/sesame>  cvs commit -m "One is Japanese, two Italian"
cvs commit: Examining .
Checking in Number.txt;
/Users/dave/sandbox/sesame/Number.txt,v  <--  Number.txt
new revision: 1.6; previous revision: 1.5
done
```

CVS actually helped us discover a misunderstanding. We resolved the conflict, and everyone's happy. Optimistic locking may actually deserve its name. And, just to make things even less scary, we need to emphasize that conflicts rarely happen on real projects.

However, it's also worth noting that CVS is not a mindreader. It might happen that two people fix the same bug in two different ways. If these changes don't conflict at the source code level, CVS will happily accept both, even though it may make no sense to have both fixes in the same code. The lack of a conflict means that you haven't trodden on anyone else's changes at the textual level, but you should still rely on unit tests to verify that the change works.

That's all for our quick tour around CVS. However, you may want to leave your sandbox repository lying around. Later on, you might find it helpful if you want to experiment with a particular facility before doing it for real in the project repository.

Chapter 4

How To...

Even though version control sounds great in theory, many teams don't use it. Sometimes this is because the theory doesn't seem to translate into practice too well. It's all very well reading a document that says something like "generate a release branch," but what does that actually mean when it comes down to typing in the correct CVS commands?

Another problem is that teams sometimes embrace version control too vigorously, creating very complex structures to hold their source, with correspondingly frightening lists of instructions for achieving even the simplest task. The result? Eventually (and in our experience that means very quickly) the team gives up; using the version control system is seen to be just too much hassle.

The remaining chapters in this book address both of these problems. They present a simple way to organize your version control system, and a set of basic practices for doing the everyday things that a team needs to do. We suggest that to start out you use these basic practices as a set of recipes; follow them whenever you need to achieve a certain result. Try hard not to deviate too much from them; if you find yourself wanting to create a scenario we don't cover, think hard before proceeding. Perhaps you don't really need it.

As with any set of recipes, you'll soon find yourself feeling more and more comfortable following them. This is the time to start experimenting slightly. However, we suggest you don't try something new directly in a real project's repository. Instead, set up the scenario in a test repository (such as the one we set up in the previous chapter) and try things out there.

4.1 Our Basic Philosophy

We think version control is one of the three essential technical practices; every team needs to be proficient in all three (the others are Unit Testing [HT03] and Automation [Cla04]). Every team should be using version control, all the time, and for everything they produce. So we have to make it simple, obvious, and lightweight (because if we don't, people will eventually stop doing it).

Simplicity means that doing something that *should* be simple will actually be simple. Checking in all my changes is a simple (and common) operation, so the basic operation should be one or two actions. Creating a new customer release is a somewhat more complex concept, so it's OK to use a few more steps doing it, but it should still be as simple as possible.

Version control has to be *obvious*: we need to arrange things so that it is clear what we're doing, and what version of the software we're doing it to. There should be no guessing when it comes to the source.

Finally, we're describing a *lightweight* process; we don't want version control to get in the way of getting real work done.

4.2 Organizing a Version Control System

Here are our basic rules for organizing your source in a CVS repository.

(see page 51)

- Before you start, you need to establish an effective and secure way to access your repository.

(see page 59)

- Once you've gained access, there is a simple set of CVS commands that you'll be using daily.

(see page 103)

- Each project that your company develops must be available as a distinct CVS module. You should be able to check out a project's complete source from a single point.

- If projects contain subcomponents that can be worked on in isolation, or if you intend to share components between projects, these components should be stored in named modules. (see page 111)
- If your project incorporates code from third parties (vendors, or perhaps open-source projects), you need to manage this as a resource. (see page 123)
- Developers use tags to identify significant points in time, including releases, bug fixes, and the start of major code experiments. (see page 91)

Chapter 5

Accessing the Repository

Before we describe all the individual CVS techniques, there's an important first step: you actually need to be able to access the repository.

So far all our experiments have been with a local repository, one that's on the same machine as its user(s). However, this is unlikely to be an effective way of working with teams. Here you need a central repository with each user accessing it over the network from their own machine. In this section we'll discuss the various options for connecting to the repository, and give guidance on selecting the method that's right for your team.

CVS gives you a number of options for accessing a repository over a network, and this can be confusing. So, let's start with something reassuring: it doesn't much matter if you chose the wrong method to start with. The connection method doesn't affect the repository at all, so you can always switch to a different method without affecting any of your work.

Second, it's important to note that you don't have to choose a single connection method. You may have some clients connecting one way, and others connecting using a totally different method. In fact, this might well be the best way of organizing things if you have some developers in house and others accessing the repository over the Internet.

Most remote CVS repositories are accessed using one of two techniques: *pserver* or *external*. In *pserver* mode, CVS runs a server process on the repository machine, and all clients connect to it. In this way, CVS is like a web server or an ftp server: it handles the connection details and manages security. Pserver mode has some advantages:

- It is relatively simple to set up.
- It can enforce read-only users (people who can check out and update, but not commit changes).
- It supports anonymous access (a facility commonly used by open source projects to grant repository access to the unwashed masses).

However pserver mode also has some drawbacks.

- It uses its own network port, and many corporate firewalls will not allow this traffic to pass.
- It uses very weak encryption of passwords, and file contents are transmitted in cleartext.
- It requires separate administration (that is to say, if you already administer remote access for users to the repository box for other purposes, you'll be duplicating some effort with CVS users).

Because of these issues, we recommend that pserver mode only be used to provide remote, anonymous access to the repository.

Accessing the repository using the *ext* (or *external*) method works slightly differently. Here, CVS uses existing operating system commands to set up a data pipe (or tunnel) between the client and the server. The default version of external CVS uses a program called *rsh* (which stands for "remote shell"). This is somewhat unfortunate. rsh was developed back when networking meant stringing some cable across the lab and when every network user was a trusted friend. rsh is convenient, but not particularly secure; rsh traffic should never be allowed to enter your network from the public Internet.

Fortunately there's a secure and plug-compatible alternative, *ssh*. We strongly recommend that all external access to CVS repositories should be through ssh tunnels. If you want to use rsh for internal access, go ahead. Just make sure that if you're working in a hotel room and need to access your repository, you switch across to ssh. (The good news here is that because ssh and rsh are compatible, you can use both with the same working copy of the repository, as we'll see in a minute.)

So, to summarize:

1. For internal access, any method works. We recommend using ssh tunneling, simply because you may as well use a single method for all access.
2. For regular external access, use ssh tunneling.[1]
3. To provide anonymous public access to your repository, use pserver mode.

So, having decided on a connection method, how do you actually use it? To some extent that depends on the tool you're using. Here we'll show how you do it from the command line; if you use a GUI tool or IDE, consult its documentation for details for your environment.

5.1 Security and User Accounts

CVS has the concept of users: people who access and make changes to the repository. It doesn't matter whether you use pserver or ssh access, you'll have to have a user id in order to be able to access CVS.

With ssh mode, you have to be able to log in to your server using a valid user id for that server. This means that every CVS user must correspond to a user account on the server (in Unix terms, you must have an entry in the `/etc/passwd` file).

With pserver mode, you have more flexibility. You can set up accounts that correspond to server's user accounts, or you can set up the server to have CVS-specific user ids which (to some extent) are independent of the operating system's

[1] CVS also supports Kerberos and GSSAPI access, but these are rarely used in practice.

user accounts. All this mapping of user names is done by the repository administrator (using the file passwd in the repository's CVSROOT module). The details of this configuration are beyond the scope of this book. (Reader Ray Schneider wrote to remind us that there are freely available tools that help administer pserver, including cvsadmin and cvspadm.[2])

Either way, the repository administrator might be tempted to cheat and set up a single user id which everyone uses to access the repository. This works, but it's really not a good idea. One of the benefits of CVS is that it keeps track of who did what; a year from now you can look through the logs and find out who altered a certain line in a particular source file. You lose this flexibility if everyone is known to CVS as `cvsuser`.

Having separate user ids also allows the repository administrator to set up access controls for parts of the repository. For example, it might be corporate policy to give all members of a team full access to their project's code, but read-only access to other teams' code. Although setting up this kind of access control is beyond the scope of this book, you clearly need to be able to identify individual users in order to implement it; using just a single user account on the server defeats these types of access control rules.

5.2 CVSROOT: The Destination Parameter String

CVS uses something similar to a URL to specify the location of the repository. This string, sometimes called the *CVSROOT*, encodes the access type, along with the user, server, name, and location of the repository you want to use. The syntax of this string is relatively messy:

:*type*:*user*@*server*:*repository_location*

The values that you enter for the various fields depend on the type of access you want to use, ssh or pserver. We'll look at

[2]Found at `http://www.cooptel.qc.ca/~limitln/cvsadmin/` and `http://securityfoo.net/ray/projs/` respectively.

the specifics shortly. First, we have to know how to pass these values into CVS.

Passing CVSROOT to CVS Commands

Many CVS commands accept the `-d` parameter, allowing you to specify the CVSROOT explicitly. We've already seen this facility when we first created our sandbox repository.

```
work>  cvs -d ~/sandbox checkout project
```

This same technique works with the more complex client-server connection methods as well. For example, if you were connecting using the pserver method to a repository on the server `xyz.com` in the directory `/var/cvs`, and if your account on that machine was called `wilma`, you could check out using:

```
work>  cvs -d :pserver:wilma@xyz.com:/var/cvs checkout proj1
```

Remembering to enter this string every time you use CVS isn't easy. Fortunately you don't have to. When you're first setting up a workspace, or when you're using other commands that require an explicit repository location, you can save some typing by establishing a default repository to use. Command line users can do this by setting the `CVSROOT` (and possibly the `CVS_RSH`) environment variables. `CVSROOT` tells CVS the default repository to use (and is equivalent to the `-d` parameter). `CVS_RSH` tells CVS what program to use when the connection method is `:ext:`—we'll want to use ssh.

To set these environment variables in Windows, right-click My Computer, select the "Advanced" tab, and click on "Environment Variables." For a single interactive session, you can also use the shell.

```
C:\> set CVSROOT=:pserver:wilma@xyz.com:/var/cvs
```

In Unix, the solution depends on the shell you use. For bash, zsh, and their ilk, add something like the following to your .profile (the `export` command sets an environment variable globally; without it, the variable would disappear once your profile had finished executing).

```
export CVSROOT=:pserver:wilma@xyz.com:/var/cvs
```

Under the C shell, you'd use `setenv` rather than `export` to achieve the same thing.

Once you're working inside a checked-out tree, CVS automatically defaults to using the repository that holds the files in this tree.

5.3 Setting up ssh Access

Before using ssh tunneling with CVS, you'll need a working ssh setup that lets you communicate between your client machines and the CVS repository machine. You can buy commercial versions of ssh (for example from `www.ssh.com`) or use open source versions (such as `www.openssh.com`). Setting up ssh is beyond the scope of this book; for our purposes we assume that you've got it installed, and that you can log in using the command:

```
ssh -l user my.server.machine
```

In order to use ssh with CVS, you need to know your user name on the server, the name of the server machine, and the location of the repository directory on that machine. (A server can handle multiple repositories: you select the one you want to use at this stage.) Armed with this information, you can then set your CVSROOT environment variable, specifying the remote machine and repository. You specify a *type* of `ext`, telling CVS to use an external program to tunnel its way through the network. Because you're using an external program to access CVS—`ssh` in this case—you need to tell CVS which one by setting the CVS_RSH environment variable.

To access the repository `/var/repository` on the machine `my.repository.com`, logging in as the user `dave`, you'd set your environment variables as follows:

CVSROOT	:ext:dave@my.repository.com:/var/repository
CVS_RSH	ssh

In Windows, you can use the GUI to set environment variables (as described previously), or you can set the values from the command line. In Windows, the commands would be:

```
C:\> set CVS_RSH=ssh
C:\> set CVSROOT=:ext:dave@my.repository.com:/var/repository
```

In Unix, add something like the following like to your .profile:

```
export CVS_RSH=ssh
export CVSROOT=:ext:dave@my.repository.com:/var/repository
```

Once this magic is complete, all your cvs commands will automatically be tunneled through a secure, encrypted link to the server.

5.4 Connecting Using pserver

If you've decided to use pserver to access your repository, then your repository administrator will need to set up a CVS password for you on the server.

As with the ssh approach, it's probably easiest to set the `CVSROOT` environment variable to tell your client where to find the repository. This time, you'll be using the pserver access method, rather that ext. There's no need to set the `CVS_RSH` variable when using pserver.

```
CVSROOT=:pserver:dave@my.repository.com:/var/repository
export CVSROOT
```

However, before you start issuing CVS commands, you first have to log in (not surprisingly, using `cvs login`):

```
cvs login
```

You'll be prompted for a password (which will have been given to you by the repository administrator). You should only have to enter this password once, as CVS remembers it for you between sessions. If you are (rightly) concerned about the security implications of this, you can use the `cvs logout` command to make CVS forget your password. However, if you're *really* concerned about security, you should probably be using ssh tunneling anyway.

Chapter 6

Common CVS Commands

In the chapter *Getting Started* (starting on page 25) we explored CVS by creating a dummy project and experimenting with some basic commands. In this chapter we'll take this further. Here we'll be presenting a set of recipes: the CVS commands that you use to do everyday tasks.

This section is not exhaustive. Later on in this book we'll be looking at more advanced issues, such as release management, workspaces, and managing third-party code. However, the commands and techniques in this chapter should handle 90% of the work you do with CVS.

These examples assume that you have your repository up and running, and that you have your environment set up to reference that repository. In fact, that latter point is the subject of the first recipe.

6.1 Checking Things Out

The `cvs checkout` command (often abbreviated to `cvs co`) takes a portion of the repository and places it in your local workspace. (We have a lot to say about workspace management starting on page 111.)

The simplest form checks out one or more modules or submodules into local directories with the same name. The following commands check out the contents of the repository modules `client` and `server`, storing them as subdirectories of the `work/` directory.

```
~>  cd work
work>  cvs co client server
```

In the section on submodules starting on page 111, we'll show you how you can also check out just part of a directory tree. The following checks out just the files stored in and below `client/templates`, storing them in the directory tree starting at `work/client/templates`.

```
work>  cvs co client/templates
```

By default CVS checks out the head of the default branch (normally the mainline). You can override this using the `-r` or `-D` options.

The `-r` option lets you check out a specific revision. The revision can be specified using absolute version numbers (such as 1.34), or by using tags. Because CVS keeps separate revision histories for each file, it's normally pretty meaningless to check out an entire project based on absolute version numbers (version 1.34 of `File1.java` might have been created two months after version 1.34 of `File2.java`). Instead, you'll probably use tags. We'll talk about tags in more detail later, but basically they are a symbolic name you can give to the current state of a set of files. As well as tags that you create, CVS provides two "magic" tags: `HEAD` represents the most recent version in the repository, and `BASE` refers to the revision you most recently checked out into the current directory. Unless you're messing around with tags and branches (which we cover in Chapter 7), you won't have to worry about `HEAD`, as it's the default for most commands.

```
work>  cvs co -r REL_1_34 client
```

-D ⇒ *by Date*

While the `-r` tag checks files out according to their version number, the `-D` tag checks out by date. The date that follows the `-D` option can be in a variety of formats, including ISO8601, Internet e-mail standard, and various abbreviations. See Table 6.1 on the next page for details.

Once you check out a directory tree for a particular revision, that revision is "sticky." This means that all subsequent work in that checked-out tree applies to that revision. This only

Specification	Examples
ISO8601	2003-06-04
	20030604
	2003-06-04 20:12
	2003-06-04T20:12
	2003-06-04 20:12Z
	2003-06-05 20:12:00-0500
E-Mail format	Mon Jun 9 17:12:56 CDT 2003
	Mon, Jun 9 17:12:56 2003
	Jun 9 17:12:56 2003
	June 9, 2003
Relative	1 day ago
	27 minutes ago
	last monday
	yesterday
	third week ago

Table 6.1: SAMPLE DATE SPECIFICATIONS ACCEPTED BY THE CVS -D OPTION.

makes sense if the revision that you check out corresponds to a branch (such as a release branch, which we cover in depth starting on page 94). If you do a `cvs status` command on a file with a sticky tag, you'll see that tag listed.

Sticky tags are CVS's mechanism for letting you work with multiple copies of files. By associating a tag with the file, CVS knows that you're working with a file from a particular point in the past, or from a particular branch in the repository tree. Because of this, CVS knows not to do things such as overwrite the version of the file at the head of the mainline when you next check in.

If you are checking out multiple releases into the same workspace, you'll probably want to override CVS's choices of directory names (otherwise the `REL_1_34` version of client will overwrite the current version of client). You can specify the directory to check out into using the `-d` option (which in this case will put the files in a directory called `rel1.34`).

```
work> cvs co client
work> cvs co -r REL_1_34 -d rel1.34 client
```

6.2 Keeping Up To Date

If you're not the only person working on a project, the chances are pretty good that the repository is being updated by others even as you are working. It's a good idea to incorporate their changes into your working copy fairly frequently; the longer you leave it, the bigger the hassle of fixing any conflicts.[1] We typically update our working copies every hour or so throughout the day.

The `cvs update` command is issued in a working directory. It brings all files in the directory (and its subdirectories) up to date with the repository. However, by default it does not create any new directories that were added to the repository since you last checked out; to do this, add the `-d` option. The following command updates all the files and directories in the client project.

```
work>  cd client
work/client>  cvs update -d
```

You can choose to update just part of your checked-out tree. If you issue the command in a subdirectory of a project, then only files at or below that point will be updated. This may save time, but it also leaves you exposed to working on an inconsistent set of files.

You can also specify one or more individual files or directories to update by naming them on the command line.

```
work/client>  cvs update File1.java templates
```

During the update process, CVS will trace the names of all directories it enters, and will show the status of each file with significant activity. For example, the following is the logging produced when updating the directory tree containing the Pragmatic Starter Kit books.

```
StarterKit>  cvs update
? SourceCode/tmpdoc.ilg
? SourceCode/tmpdoc.toc
cvs server: Updating .
RCS file: /home/CVSROOT/PP/doc/StarterKit/pragprog.sty,v
```

[1]Frequent merges serve another purpose. If another developer is going down the wrong path, or if their changes are promising to be problematic in the long term, you'll find out sooner if you merge often. The earlier you get this feedback, the less the pain involved in fixing the problem.

```
retrieving revision 1.16
retrieving revision 1.17
Merging differences between 1.16 and 1.17 into pragprog.sty
M pragprog.sty
cvs server: Updating SourceCode
A SourceCode/CommonCommands.tip
M SourceCode/HowTo.tip
A SourceCode/Releases.tip
cvs server: Updating SourceCode/images
cvs server: Updating UnitTest
P UnitTest/DesignIssues.tip
U UnitTest/InAProject.tip
P UnitTest/Introduction.tip
cvs server: Updating UnitTest/code
U UnitTest/code/Age.java
U UnitTest/code/TestMyStack.java
U UnitTest/code/testdata.txt
cvs server: Updating UnitTest/code/rev1
cvs server: Updating UnitTest/code/rev2
cvs server: Updating UnitTest/code/rev3
cvs server: Updating util
```

Lines starting with a question mark show files that are in the local workspace that CVS doesn't know about. See Section 6.4 on page 70 for information on removing this tracing. Lines starting with "A" show files that have been added locally but not yet committed to the repository, while "M" flags files that have been locally modified. "U" and "P" show files that have been updated because their repository versions are more up-to-date than our local ones. The recipe section contains a complete list of these flag characters on page 140.

Also notice that this logging shows a file, `pragprog.sty`, that has been modified by both authors. In this case, CVS was able to reconcile the changes and update Dave's locally modified copy with Andy's changes too. Sometimes the changes overlap, and so CVS flags the file with a "C," indicating a merge conflict. See Section 6.8 on page 78 for details of handling merge conflicts.

The output from `cvs update` can be fairly verbose. You can cut down on the amount of tracing using the global CVS `-q` option (yes, it goes before the "update" command).

`-q` ⇒ *Quiet*

```
work/client> cvs -q update -d
```

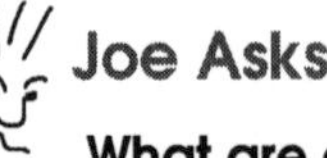

Joe Asks...

What are all these CVS options?

In some ways, CVS is more like a subsystem than a single command. When you type (say):

```
cvs checkout
```

the initial "`cvs`" identifies that you're talking to CVS, and the "`checkout`" identifies the subcommand that you want to execute.

Because of this, CVS has two separate places where you can specify options. Options that are global to the CVS subsystem (such as the `-d` option that specifies the location of the repository, and `-q`, which asks for a less logging) have to appear immediately after the `cvs` command. Options that are specific to a particular subcommand appear after that subcommand's name. One such specific option is `-d` flag of the `checkout` subcommand, which overrides the default destination of the checkout. Thus the following CVS command will check out quietly from the repository at `/usr/repository`, storing the result in the directory `temp`.

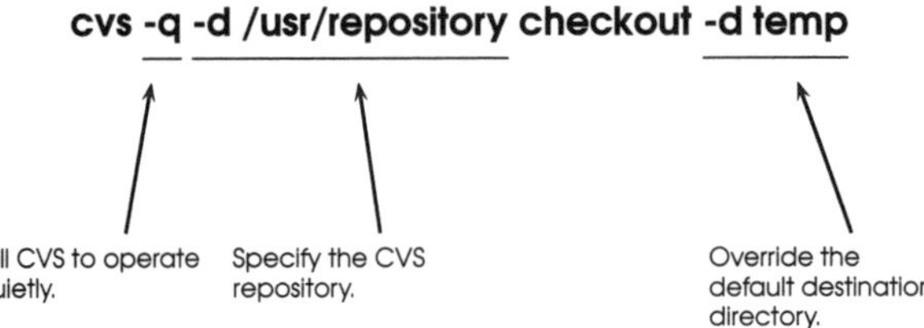
cvs -q -d /usr/repository checkout -d temp
Tell CVS to operate quietly.
Specify the CVS repository.
Override the default destination directory.

6.3 Adding Files and Directories

The `cvs add` commands tells CVS that files and directories should be added to the repository.

```
proj> mkdir timelib
proj> cvs add timelib
Directory /Users/.../proj/timelib added to the repository
proj> cd timelib
proj/timelib> #.. create and edit file Time.java ...
proj/timelib> cvs add Time.java
cvs add: scheduling file 'Time.java' for addition
cvs add: use 'cvs commit' to add this file permanently
```

If you want, you can add a creation message using the `-m` option (although that's not very common). More useful is the `-kb` option, used to flag a file as binary.

CVS and Binary Files

CVS is designed to deal primarily with files that contain text: programs, XML, and so on. This means it can do some clever things:

- It can store each revision as a set of changed lines, rather than storing the whole file for each change.
- It can deal with the differences in line endings between operating systems (in particular the newline versus carriage return/newline difference between Unix and DOS or Windows).
- It can add annotations to files by substituting certain keywords (a feature that we don't recommend using, see the sidebar on the following page).

However, give CVS a binary file to manage (a DLL, perhaps, or a Word document), and these features cause things to break.

- The tools that CVS uses to calculate the differences between revisions don't work on binary files.
- Binary files don't have line endings as such. Changing every occurrence of a byte containing a newline to two bytes containing a carriage return and a newline will probably break the file.

Joe Asks...

Why Not Use CVS's Keywords?

If you use certain "magic" sequences, things such as `$Author$` and `$Log$`, CVS will augment them with additional text each time you check the file out. The `$Author$` keyword will be changed to include the name of the person who committed the revision you're fetching. The `$Log$` keyword will prompt CVS to insert a full log of the changes to the file into the file itself.

Initially, this seems like a good idea: you're adding documentation to the file, and it costs you no effort. What could be wrong with that?

There are three problems with keyword expansion, one philosophical, and two practical.

The philosophical problem is that you're duplicating information. Everything that can be inserted using keywords is already stored within CVS (it has to be, otherwise CVS couldn't add it in the first place). So why not just go to the horse's mouth and ask CVS directly? That way you'll get authoritative information that's guaranteed to be up to date.

The second problem is that all this extra stuff in the source files gets in the way of reading the code. We've seen source with two or three full pages of log messages at the top of it, all before you get to a single line of real code. Code is there to be read, and anything that gets in the way of reading it is bad.

The third problem is that once you have keywords in CVS files, it becomes awkward to merge changes between different branches, or move files between repositories. You have to remember to use the right options at the right times, and somehow that always seems to get forgotten just before a major release.

So, keyword expansion really doesn't have many benefits, and it has several drawbacks. We recommend not using it.

- If a binary file happens to contain a sequence that looks like a CVS keyword, it would be wrong to expand it; again, you'd likely break the file's format.

To deal with this, CVS has a hack. If you specify the -kb option when you add a file, you're telling CVS to treat the file as binary. It stores complete copies of the file at each revision, and does no end-of-line or keyword processing. So, when adding a binary file, it is important to remember to use the -kb flag.

-kb ⇒ *Keyword: Binary*

```
work> cvs add -kb DataFormat.doc
```

However, just because it is important doesn't mean we always remember to do it. Fortunately, we can recover the situation.

If we realize that we didn't use the -kb option *before* we check in, we will have to re-add the file, this time with the correct flag. This is slightly tricky, because before adding it a second time we have to remove it, and we can't remove it while the file still exists in my working directory. To get around this, we have to rename the file temporarily using the Unix mv command. (The Windows equivalent is ren.)

```
work> cvs add DataFormat.doc    #<-- forgot the -kb option
cvs add: scheduling file 'DataFormat.doc' for addition
cvs add: use 'cvs commit' to add this file permanently
work> mv DataFormat.doc Temp.doc
work> cvs remove DataFormat.doc
cvs remove: removed 'DataFormat.doc'
work> mv Temp.doc DataFormat.doc
work> cvs add -kb DataFormat.doc    #<-- use the option
cvs add: scheduling file 'DataFormat.doc' for addition
cvs add: use 'cvs commit' to add this file permanently
work> cvs commit -m "Add new data format document"
```

If we realize our mistake only after we've checked the file in, things get a little trickier. The safest way to fix this is to change the flag in the repository, and then update the repository with a known, working copy of the binary file. Let's say that we incorrectly committed DataFormat.doc without the -kb flag. Here's what we'd do.

```
work> # reset the flag in the repository
work> cvs admin -kb DataFormat.doc
work> # then reset the flags in our workspace
work> cvs update -A DataFormat.doc
work> # copy a known good copy over this file
work> cp ~/docs/DataFormat.doc DataFormat.doc
work> # and save this back in the repository
work> cvs commit -m "Reset -kb flag"
```

If you spend a lot of time dealing with binary files, you might want to investigate the `cvswrappers` facility, which allows you specify to CVS the characteristics of files based on their names. We cover this in the next section, but you can safely skip this if you want.

File Characteristics and `cvswrappers`

The CVS wrapper facility allows you to set the default characteristics of files based on their file names.[2] You can specify wrappers in three ways:

1. In the file `CVSROOT/cvswrappers` in the repository.
2. In a per-user `.cvswrappers` file (note the leading dot). This file must be stored in your home directory. To us, this seems like a questionable practice; if a set of file names should be treated specially, then it makes sense to do it globally for the repository, and not just for one user of the repository.
3. Via the `-W` command line option to the `cvs import` and `cvs update` commands. This is useful for one-offs, particularly when importing existing trees.

In all cases, you specify a pattern that matches one or more filenames, and then the CVS options you want to use for files whose names match that pattern. For example, you may be about to import an existing source tree that contains a large number of Java `.jar` files and Microsoft Word documents. Both types of files are binary, and should be added with the `-kb` option.

`-W` ⇒ *Define wrapper*

We could handle this in a couple of ways. If this was the only time we were likely to be adding these types of file to our repository, you could use the `-W` option to `cvs import`. You'd have to specify `-W` twice on the command line, once for each pattern to match. There's also some fairly arcane escaping to be done to get the various quotation marks and

[2] The wrappers facility lets you do more than this. For example, you can also specify the names of programs to filter files as they pass in to and out of the repository. All this additional functionality is beyond the scope of this book.

asterisks to pass cleanly from the command line into CVS. For our particular shell, the command would look something like the following.

```
myproj>  cvs import -W "*.jar -k 'b'" -W "*.doc -k 'b'" \
                -m '' myproj ...
```

The problem with using the -W option is that it's easy to forget to use it the next time you import something. Because of this, you might want to look at setting the options permanently in the cvswrappers file, stored in the repository under CVSROOT. First, check out the CVSROOT files.

```
tmp>  cvs co CVSROOT
cvs checkout: Updating CVSROOT
U CVSROOT/checkoutlist
U CVSROOT/commitinfo
U CVSROOT/config
U CVSROOT/cvswrappers
U CVSROOT/editinfo
U CVSROOT/loginfo
U CVSROOT/modules
U CVSROOT/notify
U CVSROOT/rcsinfo
U CVSROOT/taginfo
U CVSROOT/verifymsg
```

Now change into the checked-out CVSROOT directory and edit the file cvswrappers. To add the -kb option to .jar and .doc files, add the following two lines to the end of the file using your favorite editor.

```
*.jar  -k 'b'
*.doc  -k 'b'
```

Now commit these changes back to the repository.

```
tmp/CVSROOT>  cvs commit -m "Make all .doc/.jar files binary"
cvs commit: Examining .
Checking in cvswrappers;
/Users/dave/sandbox/repo/CVSROOT/cvswrappers,v  <--  cvswrappers
new revision: 1.2; previous revision: 1.1
done
cvs commit: Rebuilding administrative file database
CVSROOT>  cd ..
tmp>  cvs release -d CVSROOT
U cvsignore
U cvswrappers
U loginfo
U modules
You have [0] altered files in this repository.
Are you sure you want to release (and delete) directory 'CVSROOT': yes
```

6.4 Ignoring Certain Files

During development, we generate lots of intermediate files. C programmers generate object files, Java programmers generate class files, and we all generate the ubiquitous temporary files. Transient files such as these should not be stored in the repository; they should be rebuilt from the source files when needed. However, if you just leave them lying around, CVS will complain about them every time you do an update or a commit.[3] Fortunately there's a simple way to tell CVS not to bother with certain files.

If a directory contains a file called `.cvsignore` (note the leading "dot"), CVS will read its contents as a list of files to be ignored in that directory. Each line in the `.cvsignore` file can be a single file name or a pattern that matches multiple files. For example, if you're working in the `client` directory and you want CVS to ignore a temporary source file, `Dummy.java`, along with all class and log files, you could create a `.cvsignore` file containing the following lines:

File `.cvsignore`:

```
Dummy.java
*.class
*.log
```

You then have an option. If you check the `.cvsignore` file in to CVS, other developers will ignore the same set of files in this directory the next time they check out. If you don't check it in, then the rules it contains will apply just to you. In general we recommend checking in `.cvsignore` files; it means that everyone is working with the same environment.

```
work/client>  cvs add .cvsignore
work/client>  cvs commit -m "Ignore Dummy, log, class files" \
                     .cvsignore
```

[3]"Complain" is probably too strong a term. CVS will list the names of the files with a question mark next to each, indicating its bemusement that someone would have files lying around that it doesn't know about.

6.5 Renaming Files

Taking a tip from the elephant family, CVS never forgets. Most of the time this is a good thing, but it can be a pain when it comes to renaming files (and, as we'll see, it's an even bigger pain when it comes to renaming directories).

You can't directly rename a file using CVS. Instead, you rename a working copy of the file in your local workspace, tell CVS to remove the old file from the repository (using `cvs remove`), and then add the file back under the new name.

For example, let's assume that we want to rename our file `Contacts.java` to `ContactMgr.java`. We need to go through the following steps:

```
proj>  cvs -q update -d
proj>  mv Contacts.java ContactMgr.java
proj>  cvs remove Contacts.java
cvs remove: scheduling 'Contacts.java' for removal
cvs remove: use 'cvs commit' to remove this file permanently
proj>  cvs add ContactMgr.java
cvs add: scheduling file 'ContactMgr.java' for addition
cvs add: use 'cvs commit' to add this file permanently
proj>  cvs commit -m "Rename Contacts.java to ContactMgr"
cvs commit: Examining .
cvs commit: Examining timelib
RCS file: /Users/dave/sandbox/proj/ContactMgr.java,v
done
Checking in ContactMgr.java;
/Users/.../proj/ContactMgr.java,v <-- ContactMgr.java
initial revision: 1.1
done
Removing Contacts.java;
/Users/.../proj/Contacts.java,v <-- Contacts.java
new revision: delete; previous revision: 1.6
done
```

There are a couple of side effects of doing this. The first is that the new file starts again at revision 1.1. All the previous revision history stays with `Contacts.java`; the file `ContactMgr.java` starts off with a clean slate.

The reason for this is that `Contacts.java` is actually still in the repository; it's just been moved into a special area (called the Attic) where it won't participate in CVS operations. As of revision 1.7, the file no longer exists. However, remember that one of CVS's jobs is to act as a time machine. If I want to build the software as it was yesterday, I expect to see the file `Contacts.java` magically reappear.

Because the file with the new name starts at revision 1.1, it won't contain the history that the file with the original name had. To get to this history (the log messages, changes, and so on) you'll need to tell CVS to look at the original name.

Similarly, even though the file is no longer in our workspace, we can ask CVS for its status. The result tells us that the file is not in our workspace and that as of version 1.7 it has been shuffled off into the Attic.

```
proj> cvs status Contacts.java
=====================================================
File: no file Contacts.java            Status: Up-to-date

   Working revision:    No entry for Contacts.java
   Repository revision: 1.7 /Users/.../proj/Attic/Contacts.java,v
```

Let's try checking out revision 1.6 (the last version where it actually existed).

```
proj> cvs update -r1.6 Contacts.java
U Contacts.java
proj> cvs status Contacts.java
=====================================================
File: Contacts.java     Status: Up-to-date

   Working revision:    1.6 Thu Jun 12 23:57:33 2003
   Repository revision: 1.6 /Users/.../proj/Attic/Contacts.java,v
   Sticky Tag:          1.6
   Sticky Date:         (none)
   Sticky Options:      (none)
```

It comes back successfully, as we'd hoped. However, it is an anachronism in a workspace that contains otherwise up-to-date files, so let's use the -A option of cvs update to tidy things up. The -A option effectively brings a workspace back into the state it should be in according to the repository.

-A ⇒ *clearAll flags*

```
proj> cvs update -A
cvs update: Updating .
cvs update: warning: Contacts.java is not (any longer) pertinent
cvs update: Updating timelib
```

What happens if sometime later we create a new file and call it Contacts.java, just like the deleted one? That won't faze CVS at all; it'll just add it to the repository with the next available revision number for that file (1.8). If you subsequently ask CVS for revisions prior to 1.7, you'll get the old version (stored in the Attic). If you ask for later revisions (or if you just use the default latest revision) you'll get the new file.

6.6 Renaming a Directory

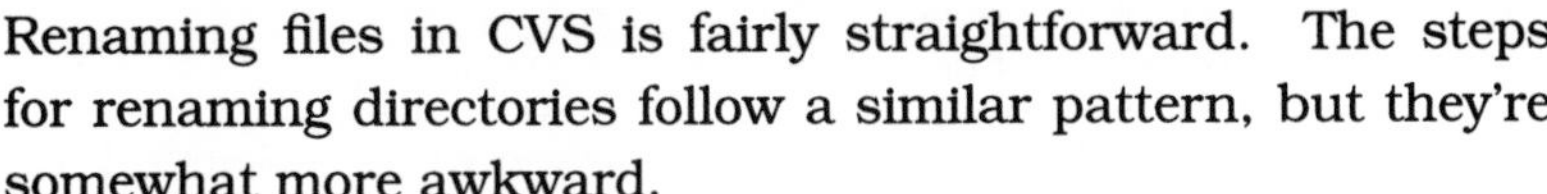

Renaming files in CVS is fairly straightforward. The steps for renaming directories follow a similar pattern, but they're somewhat more awkward.

1. Create the new directory.
2. Add the new directory to CVS.
3. Move the files from the old directory to the new.
4. Use `cvs remove` in the old directory to tell CVS that the files are no longer there.
5. Use `cvs add` in the new directory to add the files there.
6. Commit the changes, and do a `cvs update` with the `-P` option to remove the old directory from your workspace. (The `-P` option prunes empty directories.)

`-P` ⇒ *Prune directories*

We'll illustrate this by renaming the directory `timelib` (which contains the single file `Time.java`) to `timelibrary`. In this example, we'll use the Unix shell commands `mkdir`, `mv`, and `ls`, which create directories, move files, and list directory contents respectively. Under Windows, the command to create a directory is also called `mkdir`. The `ren` command renames files, and `dir` lists directory contents.

```
proj>  mkdir timelibrary
proj>  cvs add timelibrary
Directory /Users/.../proj/timelibrary added to the repository
proj>  mv timelib/Time.java timelibrary
proj>  cvs remove timelib/Time.java
cvs remove: scheduling 'timelib/Time.java' for removal
cvs remove: use 'cvs commit' to remove this file permanently
proj>  cvs add timelibrary/Time.java
cvs add: scheduling file 'timelibrary/Time.java' for addition
cvs add: use 'cvs commit' to add this file permanently
proj>  cvs commit -m "Rename timelib/ to timelibrary/"
cvs commit: Examining .
cvs commit: Examining timelib
cvs commit: Examining timelibrary
Removing timelib/Time.java;
/Users/dave/sandbox/proj/timelib/Time.java,v  <--  Time.java
new revision: delete; previous revision: 1.1
done
RCS file: /Users/.../proj/timelibrary/Time.java,v
done
Checking in timelibrary/Time.java;
/Users/.../proj/timelibrary/Time.java,v  <--  Time.java
initial revision: 1.1
done
```

```
proj> cvs update -P
cvs update: Updating .
cvs update: Updating timelib
cvs update: Updating timelibrary
proj> ls
CVS             ContactMgr.java Numbers.txt     timelibrary
```

Clearly this is not an optimal process; lack of built-in support for renaming is one of CVS's biggest weaknesses.

There's another minor annoyance. If someone comes along in the future and checks out a fresh copy of our project, they'll get `Time.java` correctly appearing in `timelibrary/`. However, they'll also get an empty `timelib/` directory, a place holder for the deleted files. You can remove this by doing a `cvs update` with the `-P` option, or by using `-P` on the original checkout.

6.7 Seeing What's Changed

The `cvs diff` command allows you to view the differences between versions of files. You can compare the version of a file in the repository with your locally modified copy, and you can see the differences between two versions of a file in the repository.

The simplest version of `cvs diff` shows you the changes you've made to a file or files.

```
work/client> cvs diff File1.java
Index: File1.java
===================================================================
RCS file: /Users/dave/sandbox/proj/File1.java,v
retrieving revision 1.2
diff -r1.2 File1.java
10c10,12
<       total += amount;
---
>       if (amount.isPositive()) {
>          total += amount;
>       }
```

This output shows that when we last checked out `File1.java` it was at revision 1.2. We subsequently edited it, adding an `if` statement around the addition.

-c ⇒ Context diff

Some folks find *context diffs* easier to read; they show not just the change, but a section of the file before and after the change was made. Just add the `-c` flag.

```
work/client> cvs diff -c File1.java
Index: File1.java
===================================================================
RCS file: /Users/dave/sandbox/repo/proj/File1.java,v
retrieving revision 1.2
diff -c -r1.2 File1.java
*** File1.java  2003/06/10 19:52:36     1.2
--- File1.java  2003/06/10 19:53:20
***************
*** 7,13 ****

      public void addInterestPayment(Money amount) {
!         total += amount;
      }

--- 7,15 ----

      public void addInterestPayment(Money amount) {
!         if (amount.isPositive()) {
!             total += amount;
!         }
      }
```

As we saw back page on page 37, there's another format for `cvs diff` listings. You can request side-by-side diffs using the option `--side-by-side`.

There's a hidden gotcha in all of these forms of `cvs diff`. The command shows the differences between the file you checked out and the file as it is now in your workspace. However, if someone has subsequently changed the file and checked those changes in, you won't see them in the diff. We'll see how to handle this shortly.

Finding Differences Between Versions

We've already seen CVS's `-r` and `-D` options when we looked at the checkout and update commands. The `-r` option allows us to specify a revision or tag, and `-D` allows us to specify a date. We can use these options with `cvs diff` as well. You can specify either option once or twice. If an option is specified once, you're asking CVS to find the differences between that revision in the repository and your local working copy. If you specify the options twice, CVS lists the differences between the two revisions in the repository (your local changes are not shown in this case).

For example, on page 63 we showed an example of a `cvs update` command that generated a merge; the local copy had been changed, and so had the version in the repository. We might be curious to see just what changes had been made in the repository since we checked the file out. The message that was logged was as follows:

```
doc/StarterKit> cvs update
cvs server: Updating .
RCS file: /home/CVSROOT/PP/doc/StarterKit/pragprog.sty,v
retrieving revision 1.16
retrieving revision 1.17
Merging differences between 1.16 and 1.17 into pragprog.sty
M pragprog.sty
```

We can examine the differences using the revision numbers shown in the log:

```
doc/StarterKit> cvs diff -r1.16 -r1.17 pragprog.sty
Index: pragprog.sty
=====================================================
RCS file: /home/CVSROOT/PP/doc/StarterKit/pragprog.sty,v
retrieving revision 1.16
retrieving revision 1.17
diff -r1.16 -r1.17
211a211,216
> %
> % Place holder for Exercise package
> %
> \newenvironment{EXERCISES}{}{}
> \newenvironment{EXERCISE}{\par{}\hrulefill\\EXERCISE:\par}{}
> \newenvironment{ANSWER}{\par{}ANSWER:\par}{}
```

By specifying the two version numbers as parameters to `cvs diff`, I can see that Andy has added three stubs for exercises to the $\LaTeX$ macros that we use to format these books.

Earlier we said that a common gotcha with `cvs diff` is that it doesn't by default show you changes between your local version and the *latest* repository version. To find this out, you need to use the special tag "HEAD," which always refers to the latest repository version.

```
work/client> cvs diff -r HEAD File1.java
Index: File1.java
=====================================================
RCS file: /Users/dave/sandbox/proj/File1.java,v
retrieving revision 1.3
diff -r1.3 File1.java
10c10,12
<       total += amount;
---
>       if (amount.isPositive()) {
>          total += amount;
>       }
14,16c16
<    public Money getTotal() {
<       return total;
<    }
---
```

Diffs and Patch

If you've spent any time developing in the open source community, you'll have come across folks flinging source patches around the world. These patches are based on the same diffs that CVS can generate, which turns out to be remarkably useful.

Perhaps you're working with an open source library, and you need to make a change. The library is hosted on SourceForge,[4] which among other things provides free CVS repositories for open source developers. As a member of the public, SourceForge lets you check the source code of the project out of the repository, but because you aren't on the list of developers, you can't check changes back in.

This is where patches come in. Simply ask CVS to give you a list of all the changes you've made (using `cvs diff`). E-mail the file containing the diff output to the library's maintainer, who will be able to use the `patch` program to apply those patches to their source. The only new facility we're using here is the `-u` option to `cvs diff`. All this does is produce output in *unified* diff format. While different maintainers have their own standards for submitting patches, and some like context diffs (`-c`), the majority seem to prefer unified diffs (`-u`).

`-u` ⇒ *Unified diff*

The following command creates a file called `diff.list` containing all the diffs that have been made to files in or below the directory `oslibrary`:

```
oslibrary>  cvs diff -u >diff.list
```

You can then e-mail this file to the maintainer, who can apply these patches to his or her version of the source using a magic incantation:[5]

```
oslibrary>  patch -p0 <diff.list
```

Patches are useful outside the context of open source. You can use patches to send suggested changes to other mem-

---

[4] `http://sourceforge.net`

[5] It's a magic incantation because we don't have the space to explain it here. You'll probably want to spend some time studying the documentation for the `patch` command if you want to start using it to apply diffs to your own source.

bers of your project team. If your clients have your source code, you can even use patches to distribute those three-in-the-morning urgent fixes that seem to crop up from time to time. Just remember to check in the changes you've made into the repository as well.

6.8 Handling Merge Conflicts

CVS doesn't lock files: everyone in a project can edit any file at any time. This one feature of CVS seems to give some people sleepless nights. "What stops two people editing the same file at the same time?" they ask. "Won't work get lost?" The simple answers are "nothing, and no." If they edit different parts of that same file, CVS will happily merge the two changes together, and life carries on.

Sometimes, however, two people edit the *same* parts of the same file (although it happens far more rarely than you might first think). When that happens, CVS cannot automatically perform a merge: it wouldn't know whose changes to keep. In these cases, CVS declares that the two versions of a file conflict and passes the matter back to a human (you) to solve.

To illustrate a conflict, we'll use our old friend Numbers.txt again. This time, we'll check it out into two separate workspaces.

```
work>  cvs co -d proj1 project
cvs checkout: Updating proj1
U proj1/Numbers.txt
work>  cvs co -d proj2 project
cvs checkout: Updating proj2
U proj2/Numbers.txt
```

In the proj1 directory, we'll change line 1 of Numbers.txt, so that the file now contains the following:

File Numbers.txt:

```
ONE
two
three
```

We'll then check this change in.

```
proj1>  #... edit ...
proj1>  cvs commit -m "Make 'one' uppercase"
cvs commit: Examining .
Checking in Numbers.txt;
```

```
/Users/dave/sandbox/proj/Numbers.txt,v  <--  Numbers.txt
new revision: 1.2; previous revision: 1.1
done
```

Now we'll bop over to proj2. Remember that we want to create a merge conflict, so we'll pretend that we don't know that someone changed the file we're about to work on. In proj2 we'll alter Numbers.txt, changing line one to be "One."

```
proj2> cvs commit -m "Capitalize 'One'"
cvs commit: Examining .
cvs commit: Up-to-date check failed for 'Numbers.txt'
cvs [commit aborted]: correct above errors first!
```

So far, so good. We can't check in until we're up to date, so we do a cvs update.

```
proj2> cvs update
cvs update: Updating .
RCS file: /Users/dave/sandbox/proj/Numbers.txt,v
retrieving revision 1.1
retrieving revision 1.2
Merging differences between 1.1 and 1.2 into Numbers.txt
rcsmerge: warning: conflicts during merge
cvs update: conflicts found in Numbers.txt
C Numbers.txt
```

CVS is telling us two things here: there's a conflict in the merge, and it's now our job to fix it.

Fixing a Conflict

The first question to be answered when fixing a merge conflict is, "why did this happen in the first place?" This isn't an issue of blame, but it often is one of communication. What are two developers doing editing the same lines of code in the same file at the same time?

Sometimes there's a good reason. Perhaps they both discover the same bug at the same time and both decide to fix it. Or perhaps they're both adding functionality which uses a common data structure, and both add fields to that structure at the same time. These are reasonable changes, and they might lead to a conflict.

But often conflicts happen because folks aren't doing a good job of letting others know what's going on. So, we strongly recommend that if you come across a merge conflict without a sensible explanation you make a point of mentioning it at the next team meeting. The goal here is to discuss the cause, and to come up with ways of improving communication so that the chances of something similar happening in the future are reduced.

Now that's all fine, but you're still left with a conflict. CVS marks these in the local copy of the file using sequences of >>> and <<< characters.

File `Numbers.txt`:

```
<<<<<<< Numbers.txt
One
=======
ONE
>>>>>>> 1.2
two
three
```

Your local changes (the lines between `<<<<<<< Numbers.txt` and `=======`)

Changes in the repository (the lines between `=======` and `>>>>>>> 1.2`)

Here we can see our new change (the "One") along with the original change ("ONE"). In many ways this is like the output of a context diff (described on page 74).

We now have to decide how to fix this. In the real world, this involves a negotiation with the other person who made the change; simply blowing their hard work away and replacing it with yours is a great way to jeopardize your invitation to the next project picnic.

The resolution could go a number of ways:

1. You decide to scrap your changes and use the version in the repository. In this case, just delete your copy of the file and do an update.

   ```
   proj2>  rm Numbers.txt
   proj2>  cvs update
   cvs update: Updating .
   cvs update: warning: Numbers.txt was lost
   U Numbers.txt
   ```

2. You decide to keep your changes and lose those in the repository. If you happen to have your version of the file in an editor buffer, simply save it back out, and then do a `cvs commit`. This version will now be in the repository. If you don't have it lying around, then you'll have to use the techniques in the next point.

Conflicts and Code Layout

While reviewing a draft of this book, Andy Oliver raised a good point about conflicts and code formatting. The problem happens like this:

Fred likes his code indented at two-character multiples, but Wilma prefers the more dramatic indentation with four-character alignment.

Fred:

```
for (i = 0; i < max; i++) {
  if (values[i] < 0) {
    process(values[i]);
  }
}
```

Wilma:

```
for (i = 0; i < max; i++) {
    if (values[i] < 0) {
        process(values[i]);
    }
}
```

One day Fred happens to be editing some of Wilma's code and decides he dislikes the indentation. He tells his editor to reindent the whole file to two-character offsets. He then makes a small change to one line, saves the file, and commits the changes back in to the repository.

The problem is that as far as CVS is concerned, every line in the file has changed. If Wilma (or anyone else) changes something, they'll get a merge conflict, because Fred's change to the indentation means that the corresponding line in the repository is different to the line in Wilma's workspace.

Now you can get around this: you can tell the `cvs diff` command to ignore changes in whitespace when calculating the difference between files using the `-b` option, for example. However, this doesn't get around the fact that you have changed the whole file, and that folks with local changes to that file will get conflicts the next time they update.

Conflicts and Code Layout (continued)

The rule is simple: don't wantonly change the layout of a shared file. If you do need to change the indentation, first make sure that no one else on the team has made local changes to the file. Then change the layout and check in the changed file. Then tell folks to update, so they'll all be working on the new version. This'll cut down on the number of conflicts people experience, and will reduce the amount of hate mail you receive.

3. If you decide that you want to use parts of both versions, then you'll need to do some manual editing. Simply edit the file that contains the conflict markers, making it look the way you want. Be sure to remove the conflict marks. For example, in our case we might decide that the first line shouldn't be "One" or "ONE," but "First."

   File `Numbers.txt`:

```
<<<<<<< Numbers.txt
One
=======
ONE
>>>>>>> 1.2
two
three
```

$\Longrightarrow$

```
First
Two
Three
```

6.9 Committing Changes

After you make a set of changes (and, in an ideal world, after you've tested that they don't break anything), you'll want to store them in the repository. We've already done this many times in this book; you simply use `cvs commit`.

However, we'd like to recommend a slightly more complex sequence of commands to follow at every commit.

```
work/project> cvs -q update -d
work/project> #... resolve conflicts ...
work/project> #... run tests ...
work/project> cvs commit -m "check in message"
```

The first line brings our local workspace in to step with the current state of the repository. This is important; although our code may work fine with the project files as they were when we last updated our workspace, other folks may have changed things that break our new code. After updating, we might have to resolve conflicts.

Even if there are no conflicts, we should then compile our code and run our tests again, fixing any problems that arise. This ensures that when we do check in we'll be checking in something that actually works in the larger project context.

Once we've checked that everything is correct, we can commit our changes, using the `-m` option to add a meaningful message. If you omit the `-m` option, CVS will bring up an editor and let you type in a longer comment. See the sidebar on the following page for suggestions on log messages.

6.10 Examining Change History

You can look at the log messages that you and your team have entered using the `cvs log` command.

```
doc/StarterKit>  cvs log pragprog.sty
RCS file: /home/CVSROOT/PP/doc/StarterKit/pragprog.sty,v
Working file: pragprog.sty
head: 1.5
branch:
locks: strict
access list:
symbolic names:
keyword substitution: kv
total revisions: 5;    selected revisions: 5
description:
----------------------------
revision 1.5
date: 2003/06/01 13:34:54;  author: dave;  state: Exp;  lines: +30 -5
Added support for colors in code and files.
----------------------------
revision 1.4
date: 2003/05/30 18:30:44;  author: andy;  state: Exp;  lines: +17 -1
Fixed up spacing of callout macros.
----------------------------
revision 1.3
date: 2003/05/30 16:21:44;  author: andy;  state: Exp;  lines: +2 -0
Added convenient \CF macro (we can rename this if you want)
----------------------------
revision 1.2
date: 2003/05/30 13:25:58;  author: dave;  state: Exp;  lines: +32 -0
Fix problem with embedding files.
----------------------------
revision 1.1
date: 2003/05/30 03:48:34;  author: dave;  state: Exp;
Initial load
```

Meaningful Log Messages

What makes a good log message? To answer this question, imagine that you were another developer coming to this code base a couple of years from now. You are puzzling over a particular piece of the system, trying to work out why something is done a certain way. You notice that changes were made in this area, and hope that the log messages will give you hints as to the motivation for the particular design chosen.

Now, back to the present. What little breadcrumbs can you drop in to the log messages today to help your fellow developers a couple of years from now?

Part of the answer comes from realizing that CVS already stores the actual details of the changes you made to the code. There's no point in writing a log message that says "Changed timeout to 42.", when a simple diff could show that `setTimeout(10)` became `setTimeout(42)`. Instead, use the log message to answer the question "why?"

```
If the round-robin DNS returns a machine that
is unavailable, the connect() method attempts
to retry for 30mS. In these circumstances our
timeout was too low.
```

If a change is being made in response to a bug report, include the tracking number in the log message: the description of the problem is already in the bug database, and doesn't need to be repeated here.

Finally (and perhaps controversially), we feel that it is perfectly acceptable to use blank log messages, but only when there's nothing meaningful to say. For example, as I type this document, I stop and format it every 30 minutes or so. If it succeeds, I check it in for safekeeping. There's nothing much to say here, so I just do

```
work> cvs commit -m ""
```

However, if I change something that affects the way the document is built (the common macros, for example), I'll add an explanatory log message.

You can use the -r option multiple times to select individual revisions to report upon. You can also use the -d option. One -d option reports on the latest entry before the given date, while two -d options reports on entries in the date range. A useful way of checking on activity in the last couple of days is:

```
work> cvs log -d "2 days ago" -d today
```

Line-by-line History

The cvs annotate command displays the contents of one or more files. For each line in each file it shows the latest revision number to change that line, along with the author of the change and the date the change was made.

```
doc/StarterKit> cvs ann OurColors.sty
Annotations for OurColors.sty
***************
 :          :          :
1.3    (dave 05-Jun-03): %%
1.3    (dave 05-Jun-03): %% Colors for sections and chapter titles
1.3    (dave 05-Jun-03): %%
1.3    (dave 05-Jun-03): \definecolor{SECCOLOR}{rgb}{.2, .2, .2}
1.3    (dave 05-Jun-03): \definecolor{SUBSECCOLOR}{rgb}{.2, .2, .2}
1.3    (dave 05-Jun-03): \definecolor{SUBSUBSECCOLOR}{rgb}{.1, .1, .1}
1.3    (dave 05-Jun-03):
1.4    (andy 05-Jun-03): %%
1.4    (andy 05-Jun-03): %% The rule under captions
1.4    (andy 05-Jun-03): %%
1.4    (andy 05-Jun-03): \definecolor{CAPTIONRULECOLOR}{rgb}{.4, .4, .4}
1.4    (andy 05-Jun-03):
1.6    (dave 10-Jun-03): %%
1.6    (dave 10-Jun-03): %% The color of line numbers in code listings
1.6    (dave 10-Jun-03): %%
1.6    (dave 10-Jun-03): \definecolor{LINENUMBERCOLOR}{rgb}{.4, .4, .4}
1.3    (dave 05-Jun-03):
```

This is a great tool when you're involved in software archeology; you can quickly find the patterns to changes and identify exactly which lines were changed by a particular revision.

cvs annotate takes a single -r or -D option, which can be used to specify the "as of" revision or date for the annotation.

6.11 Removing a Change

Sometimes we all make changes to code that we'd rather forget about.

If the change is a set of changes in our local workspace that have yet to be checked in, then we can simply delete those files in the workspace and update from the repository.

If the change is already committed, CVS can help us remove it. There are a number of ways of doing this; here we'll show a sequence of steps that we consider to be the simplest and least error prone. For this example, let's assume we're working on a contact management system. We've been making preliminary releases to beta sites, and things have been going well until a client phones up in a panic; when they removed a client contact from their address list, it removed all the client's information from the database too.

The first step is to make sure we're up to date.

```
proj> cvs -q update -d
```

Then we identify the exact revision that we want to remove. `cvs log` is useful for this. Let's have a look at the log for the main contact manager class.

```
proj> cvs log Contacts.java
RCS file: /Users/dave/sandbox/proj/Contacts.java,v
Working file: Contacts.java
head: 1.5
branch:
locks: strict
access list:
symbolic names:
keyword substitution: kv
total revisions: 5;     selected revisions: 5
description:
Manage contact list
----------------------------
revision 1.5
date: 2003/06/11 16:36:17;  author: dave;  state: Exp;  lines: +2 -0
Reformat PMB addresses
----------------------------
revision 1.4
date: 2003/06/11 16:35:40;  author: fred;  state: Exp;  lines: +1 -0
Remove client from db too
----------------------------
revision 1.3
date: 2003/06/11 16:35:11;  author: jane;  state: Exp;  lines: +2 -0
Sort clients into alpha order (CR:142)
----------------------------
revision 1.2
  :          :           :           :           :           :
```

Revision 1.4 looks suspicious, so we use `cvs annotate` or `cvs diff` to see exactly what changed between revisions 1.3 and 1.4.

```
proj> cvs diff -c -r1.3 -r1.4 Contacts.java
Index: Contacts.java
===================================================================
RCS file: /Users/dave/sandbox/proj/Contacts.java,v
retrieving revision 1.3
retrieving revision 1.4
diff -c -r1.3 -r1.4
*** Contacts.java       2003/06/11 16:35:11     1.3
--- Contacts.java       2003/06/11 16:35:40     1.4
***************
*** 15,20 ****
--- 15,21 ----
      public void removeClient(Client c) {
         clientList.remove(c);
+        database.deleteAll(c);
      }
```

This looks like the problem. However, before we start wantonly hacking someone else's change, let's do some investigating. Looking at the log, we see that this particular change was made by Fred, so we wander over and chat. It turns out that this was a simple misunderstanding; Fred hadn't realized that the call would delete all the client records. It's OK to remove the change.[6]

We now have to remove the changes to `Contacts.java` that were made between revisions 1.3 and 1.4. Let's look at the command first.

```
proj> cvs update -j1.4 -j1.3 Contacts.java
RCS file: /Users/dave/sandbox/proj/Contacts.java,v
retrieving revision 1.4
retrieving revision 1.3
Merging differences between 1.4 and 1.3 into Contacts.java
```

The `-j` option tells CVS that you want to merge changes into the current working copy. When we specify two `-j` options, we tell CVS to merge the changes between those two revisions. Then we do something neat: we specify the revisions in reverse order (1.4 comes first, then 1.3). This tells CVS to calculate the change that would be required to convert 1.4 back to 1.3, and then apply that change to our current working copy.

`-j` ⇒ *Join from*

---

[6]It would also be prudent to do a quick search of the rest of the code to see if Fred has used the `deleteAll()` call in other places.

At this point, we're back into a normal flow. We've made a change to the source, so we should test it, then commit the change back in to the repository.

```
cvs/proj> cvs commit -m "Revert deleteAll change from 1.4"
```

Reverting Bigger Changes

In the previous example we had just a single file to change. How can we handle changes that involve many files? The answer is that it depends.

One way is to apply the single file recipe to each file in turn. It's necessary to get the individual revision number of the change for each file (because CVS keeps revision numbers on a per-file, not per-commit basis).

A better way might be to anticipate changes that are likely to be controversial, and to use tags to flag them in the repository. The tags then apply to all files, regardless of their particular revision numbers. You can then use the same update trick to remove the change by using the tag names for the `-r` options.

```
proj> cvs update -j after_change -j before_change
```

Checking Your Workspace

You work in your local workspace, editing files, adding new files (and occasionally deleting files too). At the same time, other folks on your team are doing the same thing, checking their changes into the repository. As a result, it's easy to lose track of the state of your workspace. In particular, a common problem is forgetting to add new files in your workspace to the repository.

CVS provides a number of mechanisms for determining the status of the files in your local workspace. We've already seen one of these on page 62: the `cvs update` command gives the status of all the files it looks at, using a single character flag to show modified files, files that have been changed locally, files not added to the repository, and so on.

However, it's inconvenient if you have to update your workspace just to check the status of the files it contains. Fortunately, you don't have to.

The first solution is to use the `-n` option, which tells CVS not to make any changes, either to your workspace or to the repository. If you run `cvs update` with the `-n` option, it will tell you what it *would* have done, but will leave your workspace untouched. This gives you a simple listing of the status of each file. In the following example, we can see that the file `tree` in the `util` directory has not yet been added to CVS, the file `CommonCommands.tip` has been modified in the local workspace, and that two files in the `UnitTest` directory have been updated in the repository but not in our local workspace.

-n ⇒ *No changes*

```
doc/StarterKit>  cvs -nq update -d
? util/tree
M SourceCode/CommonCommands.tip
U UnitTest/FirstAssertions.tip
U UnitTest/Makefile
```

If the idea of using the `cvs update` command to check the status of files leaves you feeling nervous, reader Rick Wayne has the following suggestion:

"I'm always wondering exactly what I've mucked with in a particular source tree, and in a project of any size the output of `cvs status` quickly grows to mind-numbing proportions, with a pretty low signal-to-noise ratio. I made a `cvstat` alias on my linux box to cut the cruft:

```
~> alias cvstat="cvs status 2>&1     |
                 egrep '(\?|File:)'  |
                 grep -v Up-to-date"
```

This gives terse but useful output just on stuff that's unknown to CVS or out of sync with respect to the repository by extracting just the lines that mention file status or unknown files from the output of the `cvs status` command. For example:

```
muncher>  cvstat
? src/edu/wisc/soils/muncher/QuadtreeNodeIterator.java
File: muncher.jpx.local Status: Locally Modified
File: TestQuadtreeNode.java    Status: Locally Modified
```

Windows users would need cygwin, MKS, or some such for an `egrep` command, and might want to put the command in a batch file."

Chapter 7

Using Tags and Branches

Most of CVS is pretty simple: you update from your repository, edit files, and save the changes back after you've tested. However, many developers are put off by tags and branches. Perhaps they've worked previously in teams which abused branches, and where a diagram of the repository structure would have looked like a bowl of spaghetti rather than a controlled, linear development. Or perhaps they worked in a team where merges between branches were delayed and delayed, so that when they did finally occur it was a nightmare resolving the conflicts. Or perhaps it's just the incredible flexibility that branches offer; with so much choice, it's hard to know what to do.

In reality, tags and branches can (and should) be simple to use. The trick is to use them in the correct circumstances. In this chapter we present two scenarios where we feel that branches should be used; generating releases, and giving developers a place to experiment.

Beyond these circumstances, we suggest you think hard before adding branches to a repository. Excessive branching can quickly render any project's repository unusable.

Before we go into the specific recipes, we need to discuss tags and branches in general.

7.1 Tags, Branches and Tagging

A tag is a symbolic name. The name must start with a letter, and can contain letters, digits, hyphens, and underscores.[1] `REL_1_0`, `rev-99`, and `TRY_DT_031215` are all valid tag names, `REL_1.0`, `Bug(123)`, and `q&a` are not.

There are two types of tag. *Regular tags* give a name to the **files** in a module at a certain point of time. *Branch tags* are used to name an **entire branch** in the repository.

Regular Tags

Every file in a CVS repository has its own sequence of version numbers. A file typically starts out at version 1.1, and every time an updated version is checked in, the version number increases (1.2, 1.3, and so on). However, every file has its own sequence of numbers. If you start out a new project with three files, `file_a`, `file_b`, and `file_c`, they'll all have a version number of 1.1. However, if you edit `file_b` twice and `file_c` once, checking the source in each time, you'll end up with:

File	**Version**
`file_a`	1.1
`file_b`	1.3
`file_c`	1.2

These three files represent the current state of your application; if we were to release it now, we'd want to release version 1.1 of `file_a`, 1.3 of `file_b`, and 1.2 of `file_c`; there's no single version number that can represent the current release of the application. This is where regular tags come in. A tag creates an internal list of the version numbers currently associated with each file. For example, we could tag the current state of our repository with the tag `REL_1`. From this point forward, we could check out our source using the tag `REL_1` and get version 1.1 of `file_a`, 1.3 of `file_b`, and 1.2 of `file_c`.

You can have as many tags as you need in a repository, but tag names must be unique. For a particular file, multiple

[1]The restrictions on tag names are designed to avoid conflicts between them and (for example) revision numbers (although it's arguable that the designers of CVS went too far).

tags can refer to the same version number (so if `file_b` didn't change between now and the next release, both REL_1 and REL_2 would refer to its version 1.3).

Branch Tags

We first talked about branches on page 16, when we discussed how we can use them to handle releases in a version control system. A branch represents a fork in the history of the repository; the same file may have two or more sets of independent changes made to it, each set existing in a separate branch.

When you create a branch in CVS, you have to give it a branch tag. This tag represents the point at which the branch forks off its base codeline. When you subsequently refer to the branch tag, it's as if you were referring to the state of the files at the point the branch was created.

Tags in Practice

There are many possible uses for tags (and branches). However, excessive tagging and branching can end up being remarkably confusing. So to keep things simple, we suggest that initially you use tags for four different purposes:

Release branches. We recommend putting each release of a project onto a separate branch. The release branch tag is used to name that branch.

Releases. The release branch will contain one (and possibly more) releases: points at which the project is shipped. The release tags identify these points.

Bug Fixes. Formally reported bugs are fixed on the release branch, and (if appropriate) the fix is then merged into other release branches and the mainline. The two bug fix tags identify the point just before and just after the bug is fixed.

Developer Experiments. Sometimes a subteam has to make far-reaching changes to a project's code base. During the time that these changes are being made, the code is incompatible with the rest of the system, and will break

Thing To name	Tag Style	Examples
Release branch	RB_*rel*	RB_1_0 RB_1_0_1a
Releases	REL_*rel*	REL_1_0 REL_1_0_1a
Pre bug fix	PRE_*track*	PRE_13145 PRE_4129
Post bug fix	POST_*track*	POST_13145 POST_4129
Developer experiments	TRY_*initials_yymmdd*	TRY_DT_030631 TRY_AH_021225

Table 7.1: POSSIBLE TAG NAMING CONVENTIONS

the main build. The developers may choose to create a branch labeled with a developer experiment tag and perform their changes there.

It's a good idea to agree upon a convention for tag names with your team. Table 7.1 shows one simple scheme; this is what we'll be using in this document. In this table, *rel* stands for the release number (with punctuation converted to underscores) and *track* is a bug tracking number.

Now let's look at when you use all these different tags, and the recipes for how to use branching and tagging.

7.2 Creating a Release Branch

At intervals throughout the life of your software you'll want to generate releases. As the date for each release nears, attention will start to focus away from adding new features, instead concentrating on tidying the smaller release-specific details. Although initially the whole team may participate in this process, there'll come a time when the law of diminishing returns takes effect, and it becomes more efficient to have a release subteam focus on polishing the code for release. If this sub-

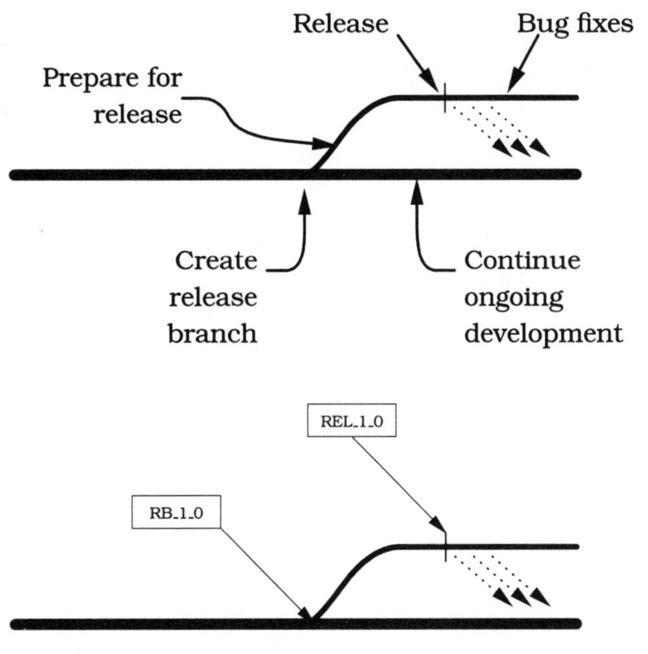

Figure 7.1: TAGGING A RELEASE BRANCH

team was working in the mainline, the rest of the team would be stalled, waiting for them to finish.

Instead, at this point in the process, move the code to be released into its own branch. While the release team works in that branch, the rest of the project can continue in the mainline. When the release itself is made, that point in the release branch is tagged with the release number. Changes made by the release team in the release branch can then be merged back in to the mainline, as shown in Figure 7.1. We've already seen the top half of this diagram when we described branches in abstract terms back on page 18. The bottom half of the diagram shows the same repository, but illustrates the tags that we're going to apply.

Create the release branch using the `cvs rtag` command. As this applies the tag to the current version in the repository, make sure everyone is checked in, so that the repository is up to date. In the example that follows, we do a `cvs commit` to ensure our workspace is checked in, then use `cvs rtag` to create a branch for release `R1.0` of the CVS module `project`.

```
work/project>  cvs commit -m ""
cvs commit: Examining .
work/project>  cvs rtag -b RB_1_0 project
cvs rtag: Tagging project
```

The `-b` option to rtag causes CVS to create a branch and give it the branch tag that we supply (RB_1_0 in this case). However, we haven't yet done anything to affect our local workspace: it is still working in the mainline. The next tip shows how to check out the release branch.

7.3 Working in a Release Branch

To access a release branch, you need to check out the project specifying the branch tag. You can do this in your current project directory (in which case you'll replace your workspace with the contents of the release), or you can do it to a separate local directory tree. We recommend the latter; it leads to less confusion, and simplifies working on both branches at the same time. To do this, we change back to our `work` directory, then check out, giving the branch tag *and* overriding the default directory name, so the source will be checked out under the directory `rb1.0`. When you check out a branch, you are checking out the most recent files in that branch; it's equivalent to the way that checking out in the mainline returns the latest development copies of the files.

```
work/project>  cd ..
work>  cvs co -r RB_1_0 -d rb1.0 project
cvs checkout: Updating rb1.0
U rb1.0/file_a
U rb1.0/file_b
U rb1.0/file_c
```

If we now edit a file in this checked out release directory and commit the changes back, we'll see that CVS adds the changes back into the branch, and not into the mainline. You can tell this from the version number that has been assigned to the changed file; it is on a branch from the mainline version 1.3.[2]

[2]The branch, which is labeled with the tag RB_1_0 has the version number 1.3.2, and the first version of the file on this branch is numbered 1.3.2.1.

```
work>  cd rb1.0
work/rb1.0>  # ... edit file_b ...
work/rb1.0>  cvs commit -m "Tidy error msg"
cvs commit: Examining .
Checking in file_b;
/Users/dave/sandbox/project/file_b,v  <--  file_b
new revision: 1.3.2.1; previous revision: 1.3
done
```

We can now continue to refine the files in preparation for the actual release.

7.4 Generating a Release

After all the tweaking is over, and the acceptance tests run, the team decides to generate a release. The most important consideration is to ensure that we tag the correct combination of files on the correct branch, so that we know precisely what's in the release.

We could use the `cvs rtag` command to do this, but that means that we have to synchronize with the rest of the team to ensure the files in the repository are stable at the time we issue the command. A better approach is to use a subtly different command. `cvs tag` tags files, just like `cvs rtag`, but uses the revisions that are checked out into a local workspace to determine how to apply the tag. The following commands create a tag for the release REL_1_0, after first running the tests on our local version and making sure we've committed all our files in to the repository.

```
work/rb1.0>  cvs update
work/rb1.0>  # ... run tests ...
work/rb1.0>  cvs commit -m "..."  # if needed
work/rb1.0>  cvs tag REL_1_0
cvs tag: Tagging .
T file_a
T file_b
T file_c
```

From now on, developers will be able to check out the code used to build this release by specifying the release tag.

```
work>  cvs co -r REL_1_0 -d rel1.0 project
cvs checkout: Updating rel1.0
U rel1.0/file_a
U rel1.0/file_b
U rel1.0/file_c
```

tag? rtag? What's up?

CVS provides two commands for tagging files and modules. What's the difference between them, and when do we use each?

The clue lies in the names: the command `cvs rtag` tags a module in the **r**epository, while plain `cvs tag` tags files based on our local workspace.

Because `rtag` uses the repository, we don't even need to be in a local workspace to use it (although if we are, it'll use that repository's Root automatically). To use `cvs rtag` you need only give a tag and a module name. The default action is to apply that tag to the current HEAD version of that module in the repository. (Having said that, you can also do a whole lot more; see the command description on page 146 for more details.)

`cvs tag` is different: you have to use it while you're in a local workspace. It applies the given tag to files as they were when you last checked-out or updated. This is significant; if you've edited a file locally, it will be eventually stored with a new version number. However if you issue a `cvs tag` command before committing, that tag will refer to the previous version. (If you use the `-c` flag, `cvs tag` will check that local files are not modified before applying the tag.)

So you should use `cvs rtag` when the tag applies to some repository-wide state (for example, when you're generating a release) and use `cvs tag` when the event is more local (for example, when you're about to fix a bug).

7.5 Fixing Bugs in a Release Branch

Bugs happen. The trick is to handle them in a controlled manner. In a release branch, this means that we need to keep track of the changes made to fix the bug, and then make sure that we apply those fixes to every other branch that might contain the same problem. The latter problem is particularly important. By their nature, branches contain duplicates of code. That means that if you find a bug in the source code in one branch, there's always the possibility that the same bug exists in another branch (after all, originally the source code was the same, bugs and all). In the case of a release branch, we need to be able to apply our fix back to the mainline. We might also need to apply it to other release branches (if they also contain the buggy code).

Without version control, this is a tricky problem. With version control, we can control the process better. We do this by getting the version control system to keep track of the source code changes made while fixing the bug, and then merging those changes in to the code in other affected branches.

Logically, the process works as follows. First, we fix the bug, using tags so we can isolate the changes we make.

- Check out a copy of the branch containing the bug into your local workspace.
- Tag the repository with a *pre-fix* tag.
- Generate a test to reveal the bug, fix the code, and verify the build.
- Commit your changes back in to the repository.
- Tag the repository with a *post-fix* tag.

Now we go in to all the other affected branches (potentially including the mainline) and merge the changes we just made in to them. The changes can be determined from the repository by asking for the difference between the pre-fix tag and the post-fix tag.

In CVS terms, we use the following recipe. These examples assume that the bug is reported in the 1.0 branch, and that we've given it the tracking number 1234.

```
work> cvs co -r RB_1_0 -d rb1.0 project
cvs checkout: Updating rb1.0
U rb1.0/file_a
U rb1.0/file_b
U rb1.0/file_c
work> cd rb1.0
work/rb1.0> cvs tag PRE_1234
cvs tag: Tagging .
T file_a
T file_b
T file_c
work/rb1.0> # create test, fix problem, validate
work/rb1.0> cvs commit -m "Fix PR1234"
cvs commit: Examining .
Checking in file_c;
/Users/dave/sandbox/project/file_c,v  <--  file_c
new revision: 1.2.2.1; previous revision: 1.2
done
work/rb1.0> cvs tag POST_1234
cvs tag: Tagging .
T file_a
T file_b
T file_c
```

We now need to apply this fix to the mainline code. To do this, we go to our mainline workspace, make sure that it is up-to-date, and then merge in the fix from the release branch. Finally, run our tests, and if they pass we commit the changes back in to the mainline.

```
work/rb1.0> cd ../project
project> cvs update
cvs update: Updating .
project> cvs update -j PRE_1234 -j POST_1234
cvs update: Updating .
RCS file: /Users/dave/sandbox/project/file_c,v
retrieving revision 1.2
retrieving revision 1.2.2.1
Merging differences between 1.2 and 1.2.2.1 into file_c
project> # ... test ...
project> cvs commit -m "Apply fix for PR1234 from RB1.0"
cvs commit: Examining .
Checking in file_c;
/Users/dave/sandbox/project/file_c,v  <--  file_c
new revision: 1.3; previous revision: 1.2
done
```

7.6 Developer Experimental Branches

Sometimes developers need to make wide-ranging changes to a project (for example to change a persistence layer, or introduce a new security mechanism). These are the kinds of changes that take a minimum of several days to code. These changes can't be introduced incrementally: they affect too much code. These changes are typically at a low level in the application, and normally have a far-reaching impact on the rest of the system.

If a single developer wants to make a wide-ranging change to the source, he or she could work in their local workspace. However, this has a couple potential downsides. First, the developer loses the benefit of version control while they're working on the change; they lose the ability to revert just sections of their work, they lose revision history, and so on. They also don't have their work in a central repository, so there's a chance that it won't be backed up.

If multiple developers are working on a wide-ranging change, then they have bigger problems; they need to be able to share changes and work on the same (experimental) code base.

The answer is to put the experimental code into a branch in the version control system. The developers working on the changes use that branch in their workspace. When they've finished their work, they can make the decision about integrating their work back in to the mainline. If they decide that experiment is a failure, they can abandon the branch. Otherwise they simply merge the changes made in the branch back in to the mainline. Whatever their decision, future work continues in the mainline, and the branch becomes history.

Creating a developer branch is effectively the same as creating a release branch. We tag the branch with an experimental tag.

```
work/project>  cvs commit -m ""
cvs commit: Examining .
work/project>  cvs rtag -b TRY_DT_030925 project
cvs rtag: Tagging project
```

This does not change the tags in the current working directory; in order to switch to the newly created branch, you need to do an update, specifying the branch tag.

```
work/project>  cvs update -r TRY_DT_030925
cvs update: Updating .
```

To return your working files to the mainline, use `cvs update` with the `-A` parameter:

```
work/project>  cvs update -A
cvs update: Updating .
```

7.7 Working With Experimental Code

When you work with an experimental code branch, you can either replace the code in your current workspace (using `cvs update` with the `-r` option) or you can check out into a separate directory tree. To be reliable, if you use the update method you need to ensure you issue the command from the top level of your directory tree.

```
work/project> cvs update -r TRY_DT_092503
cvs rtag: Updating project
```

If you decide instead to check out into a separate directory (our preferred option), remember to use the `-d` option to override the default directory name.

```
work/project> cd ..
work> cvs co -r TRY_DT_092503 -d proj_exp project
cvs checkout: Updating proj_exp
U proj_exp/file_a
U proj_exp/file_b
U proj_exp/file_c
work> cd proj_exp
```

7.8 Merging The Experimental Branch

Merging the experimental branch into the mainline uses a single `-j` tag, indicating that CVS should merge in all changes in the branch. Before issuing the command, you need to make sure that all changes in the experimental branch are checked in, and that you've moved across to a workspace in the mainline. (This little dance is the reason we recommend checking the experimental branch out into a separate directory tree).

In the example that follows, we'll assume that the directory `proj_exp` contains the experimental code and `project` contains the mainline. The merge then proceeds as follows:

```
work> cd proj_exp
work/proj_exp> cvs commit -m "Finalize changes"
work/proj_exp> cd ..
work> cd project
work/project> cvs update -j TRY_DT_092503
cvs update: Updating .
RCS file: /Users/dave/sandbox/project/file_a,v
retrieving revision 1.1
retrieving revision 1.1.4.1
Merging differences between 1.1 and 1.1.4.1 into file_a
RCS file: /Users/dave/sandbox/project/file_c,v
...
```

Chapter 8

Creating a Project

The word "project" is fairly loosely defined. One person working for a week to implement a web form can be a project, as can many hundred laboring for many years. But most projects share a set of common characteristics:

1. Each project has a name. This may sound trivial, but we tend to give things names when we want to identify them as independent entities. Names don't have to be external brands, approved by marketing and subject to field tests in major metropolitan areas. Project names are simply internal to your organization.

2. Each project is cohesive; things in the project work together to achieve some business aim.

3. The components within a project tend to be maintained as a unit; you'll release a version of the project as a whole.

4. The stuff in a project shares a common set of engineering standards and guidelines, and uses a common architecture.

It is important to consider this list when putting projects into a version control system, because it is often hard to know where to draw the boundaries between different projects. Getting the project structure wrong is a major source of frustration when using version control, and can lead to a lot of wasted effort as time goes on.

So, before creating projects in your repository, spend some time planning. For example, is your project going to implement a framework that the company will use in future development efforts? If so, then perhaps that framework should be a separate project in its own right, with your current project and those other future projects sharing in its use. Is your project developing multiple independent components? Perhaps each should be its own project. Or is your project writing an extension for an existing chunk of code? Perhaps then it should be a subproject of that original project.

8.1 Creating the Initial Project

There are basically four ways to create a project under CVS.

1. Import: Load existing source into the repository as a new CVS project.
2. Über-project: Create all your projects as sub-projects of a company-wide dummy project.
3. Clean-slate: Create an empty CVS project in the repository, check this project out in a client, then add files to it from there.
4. Copy in an existing RCS repository. RCS is an early revision control system; CVS is based on RCS.

The last two methods are rarely used in practice. The "clean-slate" approach requires having access to the repository, and there is great potential for messing things up. The "RCS copy" method is both ugly and not particularly appropriate (unless you happen to have a whole lot of code sitting in RCS). That leaves us with two options: import and über-project.

The Import Method

If you have existing source files (even if it's just the project's README file) you can use the CVS import facility to create a new project. In the examples that follow, we'll assume you're working on the *Wibble* project (the Wickedly Integrated Business to Business Lease Exchange).

You'll need a directory tree containing the files that you want to import (and only the files you want to import; be sure to clean up all the various backup files and other dross before going any further). Make sure that you're in the top-level directory of this tree (in our case, in the directory `wibble`), then issue the `cvs import` command:

```
wibble>  cvs import -m "Initial import" wibble wibble initial
```

There's a lot going on in this command, so let's look at each piece.

The `-m` option specifies the message to be logged with this import. In this case we use "Initial import."

Next comes the name of the project where we're going to place the source. In this case we use "wibble," our project's name. This project will be added to the top level of the repository.

The next two parameters are both required and superfluous. They're required because the command insists that you supply them, but they're superfluous because they don't really mean much in this context. we'll see what they're really used for when we talk about third party code on page 123. For now, just use the strings "wibble" (the project name, again) and "initial" and move on.

Your project is now checked in. You should check it out using a normal `cvs checkout` command and, if everything is OK, you can delete the original directory tree that you used for the import.

The Über-project Method

The second method for creating projects is in some ways the simplest. However, we pay for that simplicity; we have to be fairly disciplined when we use it.

In this method, your repository administrator initially creates an empty repository. From then on, to add a new project you:

- Check out the top-level of this repository. To do this, you use the regular `cvs checkout` command, but add the `-d` and `-l` options, and specify the special project name of "." (a period). The `-d` option is used to specify the directory name of the workspace, and the `-l` option tells CVS not to check out the entire repository contents; only top-level directories are created in the workspace.

- Create your new project directory in this checked-out workspace, and use `cvs add` to add it to the repository.
- Release the entire checked-out workspace (because you don't need the entire repository).
- Check out again, this time specifying the name of the project that you just created.

```
work>  cvs checkout -l -d tmp .
cvs checkout: Updating tmp
work>  cd tmp
work/tmp>  mkdir new_project
work/tmp>  cvs add new_project
Directory /Users/.../new_project added to the repository
work/tmp>  cd ..
work>  cvs release -d tmp
You have [0] altered files in this repository.
Are you sure you want to release (and delete) directory 'tmp': yes
work>  cvs checkout new_project
cvs checkout: Updating new_project
work>  cd new_project
work/new_project>  # edit ...
work/new_project>  cvs add ...
```

If you decide to use this approach, you need to be disciplined when it comes to keeping projects distinct. It is both tempting and easy to treat all the company's projects as a single big project, and to start using code (or even altering code) that doesn't really belong to your project.

8.2 Structure Within the Project

Your company may well already have standards which dictate how to organize the source code and directories within a project. If you're developing with Java, for example, you might be using the Jakarta conventions for laying out directories.[1] If you don't currently use a standard, here are some basic suggestions.

[1] `http://jakarta.apache.org/site/dirlayout.html`

Top-Level Files

README Incredible though it seems, a couple of years from now the latest red-hot project will have faded down to a dull gray, and you'll have a hard time remembering exactly *what* the Wibble project was all about. So create a file called README in the top-level project directory. Write a small paragraph describing what this project is all about: the business problems it is solving, the basic technologies used, and so on. This isn't meant to be a full description; it's just an *aide-memoir* intended to trigger those long-dormant neurons when you come back after a long absence.

BUILDING Create another top-level file called `BUILDING`. This will contain simple hints to future code archaeologists who might want to rebuild this project from source. Because you'll be automating the build, this document will be short: Figure 8.2 on page 110 shows an example.

GLOSSARY Create one more top-level file called `GLOSSARY`. Make it a habit to document all project-specific jargon in this file. Not only will this make it easier for future developers when they're trying to work out what a "wibble_channel" is, but it will also guide the project team when it comes to naming classes, methods, and variables.

Top-Level Directories

Most projects will have at least the following top-level directories.

doc/ Check all project documentation into `doc/` and its subdirectories. Don't forget to add memos and e-mails that describe decisions reached. It's normal to have directories under `doc/` which contain different document types, or for different phases of the project.

If your project relies on external documentation (for example, the description of an algorithm or a file format held on a third-party web site), consider copying this and storing it under the `doc/` directory tree (copyright permitting, of course). This will make it easier for future maintainers if the external site has since gone away. If you can't copy this material into your project, create a file in `doc/` called `BIBLIOGRAPHY` and add links and a brief description in it.

data/ Many projects carry along data (for example, information needed to populate lookup tables in the database). Keep this data in a single location (if for no other reason that someone, at sometime, will urgently need to find out why we're charging 127% sales tax in Guam).

db/ If your project uses a database, store all the schema-related stuff here. Work hard not to fall into the habit of modifying schemas online. Have your data base administrator create SQL scripts for each update—scripts that both update the schema *and* migrate the data. By keeping these in the repository, you'll be able to migrate any version of the database to any other version.

src/ The project's source code should be stored under this directory.

util/ A directory to hold various project-specific utility programs, tools, and scripts. Some teams have a directory called `tools/` instead.

vendor/ If your project uses third-party libraries or header files that you want to archive along with your own code, do it under a top-level vendor/ directory.

vendorsrc/ Sometimes a project will import and include code from a third-party (for example, if it is using an open source library and needs to ensure that it will have access to a particular version of the source for the life of the application). You'll include the binary libraries (and possibly the header files) in the `vendor` directory, but you'll also want to retain the source from which these libraries were built. Store these sources under the `vendorsrc/` directory. We have more to say about vendor source code in *Third-Party Code* starting on page 123.

A possible file layout for the Wibble project is shown in Figure 8.1 on the facing page. In this project we have all our own

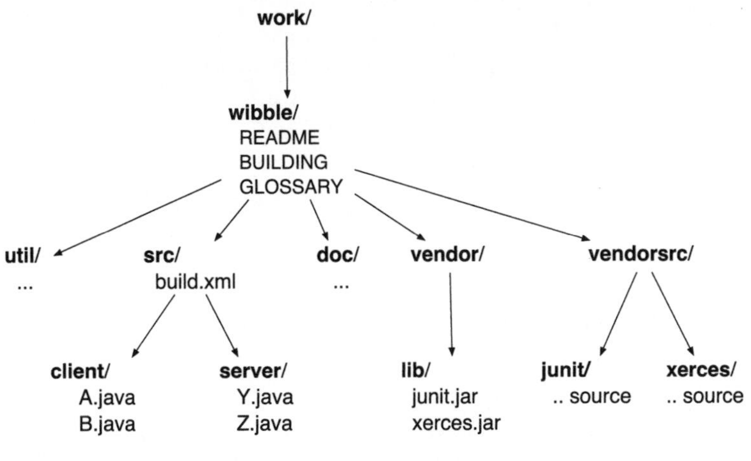

Figure 8.1: POSSIBLE WORKSPACE LAYOUT

source code (divided into client and server components) along with some imported open source code (the JUnit and Xerces frameworks).

In addition, many projects will have a standard set of directories that are used during the build or release project. These directories do not contain files that should be stored in the repository (as their contents are generated on the fly), but some teams still find it convenient to have these directories appear in every developer's workspace. To do this, you can add these empty directories to the repository; they'll appear in the workspace when developers check out.[2] (An equally valid alternative is not to store these directories in CVS. Instead, have your build scripts create them as needed, and then tidy them up when you're done with them. If you use this scheme, remember to add the directory names to your `.cvsignore` file to stop CVS complaining every time you check in or out.)

[2]Reader Maik Schmidt points out that these empty directories won't be created on check-out if the user specifies the `-P` (prune) option to the `cvs update` or `cvs checkout` commands. To avoid this problem, he creates and checks in an empty, invisible (under Unix) file into each of these directories. His convention is to use the name `.keepme` for these files.

```
Prerequisites:
  * Oracle 9.6i (perhaps later versions, but
    that configuration's not tested)
  * GCC 2.96

Building:
  ./configure [--with-oracle=<dir>]
  make
  make test
  make install

More info:
  doc/building.html
```

Figure 8.2: SAMPLE BUILDING FILE

You'll also want to keep your test code somewhere, but opinions vary wildly on where this should be. Some teams like keeping it in parallel directories to their source tree, others put the tests in subdirectories of the source files being tested. To some extent the "correct" answer depends on the language being used. For example, the Java package naming rules mean that if you want to test protected methods you'll need to construct parallel trees (or put your tests in the same directory as the source being tested). We cover this in more detail in the companion book *Pragmatic Unit Testing* [HT03].

There are no hard-and-fast rules for structuring directories in a project. However, being consistent across projects will greatly help people who come along in future, and will give you the flexibility to move between projects without experiencing that "I'm totally lost" feeling.

Chapter 9

Using Modules

Small projects are easily managed as a whole; people typically have the entire project source available in their local workspaces and tests are run across the entire project source. However, once projects (and their teams) reach a certain size, we find it useful to partition them into subprojects. The rules for these subprojects are similar to those for overall projects: subprojects should be named, cohesive, maintained as a unit, and internally consistent. The subprojects should be relatively independent of each other, and should work together to implement the overall requirement. (If they don't work together in this way, then they shouldn't be subprojects; they should be top-level projects.)

One classic division of a large project might be into client-side and server-side components. The client team works on the client subproject, and the server team works on the server code. The division into subprojects helps enforce the discipline to produce a clean interface in the software, and will help encourage the teams to produce software that is testable in isolation (so the server code will be capable of being tested without having the client code present, for example).

Other projects might be better divided horizontally; backend applications might be broken into database access code, calculation modules, external systems interfaces, and so on.

Most large projects benefit from being divided into subprojects, and most are realistically divided both vertically (as with

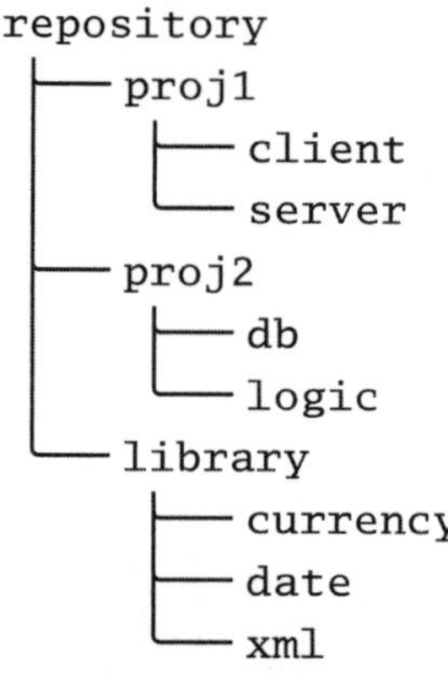

Figure 9.1: PROJECTS AND SUBPROJECTS

the client/server split) and horizontally. Spend a little time before creating a large project considering how the source code in the repository should map onto the project's architecture. Don't worry about getting it exactly right upfront; you can always adjust things as you go along. But starting with the discipline in place will make it easier to continue that way.

9.1 Subprojects the Easy Way

When you organize your source into a directory structure you will normally break subprojects into their own distinct subtrees. For example, Figure 9.1 shows a repository containing two projects and a set of common libraries. (This diagram shows the logical structure of the repository; a real repository might have more layers). The team working on project *proj1* have decided to split their code into client and server components. The *proj2* team seem to have split into layers, with a directory holding the database access code and another for the program logic. In addition, both teams have some common code that they share in the `library` tree.

In this environment, you can manually control how much of the repository you have in your local workspace. For example, you might be a developer on the client-side of `proj1`. You need the `xml` and `date` libraries to build your application.

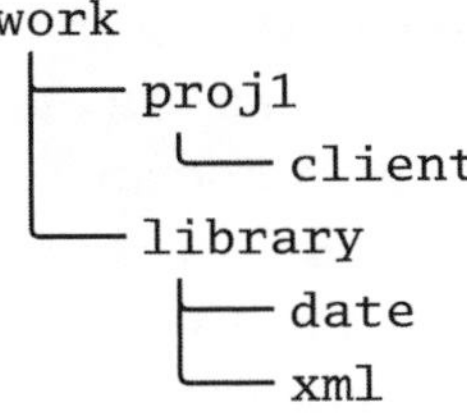

Figure 9.2: A DEVELOPER'S WORKSPACE

You could check out just these parts of the repository using commands such as:

```
work>  cvs co proj1/client
work>  cvs co library/xml
work>  cvs co library/date
```

By default, CVS checks out these parts of the repository into a directory structure that mirrors the repository. This means that our developer's workspace would look something like Figure 9.2.

It is possible to override CVS's behavior; the `cvs checkout` command takes an optional parameter which specifies the place to put the checked-out files. However, this is a feature that should be used with care. To see why, we'll need to look at how we'd go about building this project code.

Let's assume that you follow our third project recommendation and have implemented an automated build system. This system will take the project source out of the repository and run your build script to compile and link the project's source code. In order for this to work, the build script will need to know where all the source code is.

If we're just working within a single project, all the source files sit in a single directory structure, so the relative path from one component to another will always be the same. However, once we include a second module in the build life gets more interesting. Now our code has to be able to get to code in other modules. How can it do this? Different teams have come up with different solutions:

- **Customize the build environment.** Every developer must set up the parameters for their IDE to point to the appropriate directories. The automated build has the directories for that machine hard wired in. Although very common, this is a remarkably error-prone procedure. It is common to have different versions of a library checked out multiple times on the same machine (for example, if you are both working on the mainline development and also fixing a bug in a previous release). If you forget to update all the various build parameters, you could be building the new source with the old libraries, or vice-versa. And, if your project uses different operating systems during the build, this method isn't particularly portable. Relying on manual procedures like this is just not a good idea.

- **Use environment variables.** The various build scripts use environment variables to reference the tops of the various module trees, and the contents of the trees are relative references from there. This is slightly better than manually configuring your build scripts for each machine; the configuration is done once in each machine's environment. It also means that the build scripts can be checked in to the repository; the script is the same on each machine and only the environment variables change. However, it still suffers from the multiple version problem; switching back and forth between different checked-out versions of the same code is error prone.

  IDEs such as Eclipse provide support for this style of operation; you can set up machine-level configuration variables, and then reference these from each projects' build instructions.

- **Use relative paths.** Rather than having each user configure his or her machine for the build, instead arrange things so that the build environment is self-contained and identical on each box. We do this by making it a rule that the relative path between any two things in the repository remains the same when we check those things out. Another way of saying this is that the structure of the checked out source in a local workspace will always mirror the structure in the repository (although the workspace may contain just a subset of the stuff in the repository).

This is a good way of organizing things: all the build scripts know where everything else is, because the relative path will always be the same. Developers moving between machines will find the checked-out directory structure identical on each.

Because of this, we strongly recommend that you:

1. Choose a directory structure that works.
2. Use it in the repository.
3. Insist that all developers check out using this structure.

Once you have this in place, build tools will know where to find libraries and other project components, and developers can move from machine to machine without having to spend hours tracking down how each is configured.

Multi-repository Projects

CVS versions 1.11 and later allow you to check out code from multiple repositories (or from multiple locations in the same repository) into subdirectories of an already checked-out tree. If you perform an update or commit command at the top level, CVS will automatically switch between repositories as it traverses through the directory tree.

In some special cases this is a remarkably useful feature. However, in general it suffers from the same build issues that arise when checking out multiple projects from the same repository into random places in your workspace. We advise against using this facility unless your team has established a coherent set of standards which dictate where various subdirectories should be placed. Again, the objective is to aim for total consistency between all team members.

9.2 CVS Modules

CVS stores its repository in a standard file system directory tree. Until now, we've been relying on the fact that when you issue the command "`cvs co` *name*", CVS looks for a top-level directory in the repository called *name* and checks it out into your workspace. However, CVS also allows you to partition your repository into modules. In many ways modules can help you address all the problems of organizing the source in your repository into usable chunks.

A CVS module is basically a way of giving a name to one or more subdirectories in a repository. However, as with most things, there's more to it than that. CVS actually supports three kinds of module: *alias modules*, *regular modules*, and the elegantly-named *ampersand modules*. But before we look at each of these, we first need to know how to configure these modules in CVS.

CVS Configuration

You may have noticed the special directory, `CVSROOT`, that automatically appeared in the repositories that you created. This directory contains a number of CVS configuration and option files. Because this directory is present in the repository, you can check it out just like any other.

```
work> cvs -d ~/sandbox co CVSROOT
cvs checkout: Updating CVSROOT
U CVSROOT/checkoutlist
U CVSROOT/commitinfo
U CVSROOT/config
U CVSROOT/cvswrappers
U CVSROOT/editinfo
U CVSROOT/loginfo
U CVSROOT/modules
U CVSROOT/notify
U CVSROOT/rcsinfo
U CVSROOT/taginfo
U CVSROOT/verifymsg
```

Because we're concerned with configuring modules in a repository, we need to work with the file `CVSROOT/modules`. If you open this file in an editor, you'll notice it contains a whole lot of comment lines (that start with a "#" character) and nothing else. That's because our sandbox repository does not yet have

```
# Three different line formats are valid:
#       key     -a    aliases...
#       key [options] directory
#       key [options] directory files...
#
# Where "options" are composed of:
#   -i prog  Run "prog" on "cvs commit" from top-level of module.
#   -o prog  Run "prog" on "cvs checkout" of module.
#   -e prog  Run "prog" on "cvs export" of module.
#   -t prog  Run "prog" on "cvs rtag" of module.
#   -u prog  Run "prog" on "cvs update" of module.
#   -d dir   Place module in directory "dir" instead of module name.
#   -l       Top-level directory only -- do not recurse.
#
# NOTE:  If you change any of the "Run" options above, you'll have
# to release and re-checkout any working directories of these modules.
#
# And "directory" is a path to a directory relative to $CVSROOT.
#
# The "-a" option specifies an alias.  An alias is interpreted as if
# everything on the right of the "-a" had been typed on the command line.
#
# You can encode a module within a module by using the special '&'
# character to interpose another module into the current module.
# This can be useful for creating a module that consists of many
# directories spread out over the entire source repository.
```

Figure 9.3: A TYPICAL EMPTY MODULES FILE

any modules defined. (A typical empty modules file is shown in Figure 9.3.)

As an experiment, let's try defining a module. If you're working with our original sandbox repository, you should have an existing top-level directory called `sesame` already defined. Let's define a module so that we can also refer to `sesame` as `projectX`. Using an editor, add the following line to the bottom of the checked-out modules file:

```
projectX    sesame
```

Having made the change, we now need to get it back into the repository. That's simple; just commit it.

```
work/CVSROOT>  cvs commit -m "Add module projectX"
cvs commit: Examining .
Checking in modules;
/Users/dave/sandbox/CVSROOT/modules,v  <--  modules
new revision: 1.2; previous revision: 1.1
done
cvs commit: Rebuilding administrative file database
```

Notice there's some additional logging here: CVS recognizes that we've changed some configuration information and updates itself accordingly.

Now let's test that we can use `projectX` as a module name. Go back to your `work` directory and try to check it out.

```
work> cvs -d /Users/dave/sandbox co projectX
cvs checkout: Updating projectX
U projectX/Color.txt
U projectX/Number.txt
```

You should now have a subdirectory of `work` called `projectX` containing the contents of the sesame project.

Before we go any further, let's tidy up. We've checked out two modules (`CVSROOT` and `projectX`) that we won't be needing, so let's release their contents. This removes them from our workspace (but does not remove them from the repository). We'll use the `cvs release` command to do this. Specifying the `-d` option makes CVS remove our local copy of the files.

```
work> cvs -d /Users/dave/sandbox release -d CVSROOT
You have [0] altered files in this repository.
Are you sure you want to release (and delete) directory 'CVSROOT': yes
work> cvs -d /Users/dave/sandbox release -d projectX
You have [0] altered files in this repository.
Are you sure you want to release (and delete) directory 'projectX': yes
```

Having looked at the mechanics of defining modules, let's look at the kinds of modules we can create.

Alias Modules

Alias modules are simple shortcuts: "when I say *X* convert it to *Y/Z*." Use alias modules when you want to divide a repository into subprojects, and you want to ensure that people use consistent directory structures.

Remember our developer who only wanted to check out a subset of the project shown in Figure 9.1 on page 112? Using basic CVS commands, the developer would have to use the following commands to check out each individual subproject.

```
work> cvs co proj1/client
work> cvs co library/xml
work> cvs co library/date
```

For a small tree such as this example, this isn't a big problem. However, once projects start to grow, this can get onerous. This is where we can use aliases. For our sample project, we could add the following lines to our modules file:

```
client -a   proj1/client
xml    -a   library/xml
date   -a   library/date
```

Now our developer could just type:

```
work> cvs co client
work> cvs co xml
work> cvs co date
```

CVS looks up the names, and converts them into the paths in the modules file. It then checks out using these paths. This means that even though you say "cvs co xml", CVS will still put the checked-out files in the workspace directory library/xml. This way we can keep all the checked-out code in consistent places.

However, we can take this a couple of steps further. Perhaps these three portions of the tree form some meaningful group. We can turn them into a module too, so that we can now refer to them using a consistent name. In the modules file, add the line:

```
clientall  -a proj1/client library/xml library/date
```

Now our developer can check out all three subtrees using a single command.

```
work> cvs co clientall
cvs checkout: Updating proj1/client
cvs checkout: Updating library/xml
cvs checkout: Updating library/date
```

Finally, we can tidy this up. Rather than repeat the paths to the various subtrees in our modules file, we can use the individual aliases in our compound alias, leading to the following four lines (and diagrammatically in Figure 9.4 on the next page).

```
client     -a   proj1/client
xml        -a   library/xml
date       -a   library/date
clientall  -a   client xml date
```

Regular Modules

While alias modules allow you to define short names for existing subtrees in the repository, regular modules allow you to rename a section of the tree as you check it out. For exam-

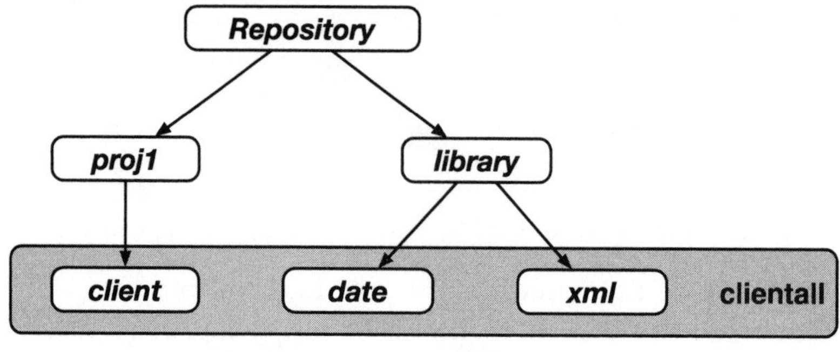

Figure 9.4: MODULES AND ALIASES

ple, you could define a module using the following line in the modules file:

```
clnt   proj1/client
```

If you then check out using that module name, CVS will ignore the path of the files in the repository and instead check out into the directory `clnt`. A file such as `proj1/client/README` will be checked out into `clnt/README`.

Now earlier we went on about how this kind of moving of directories is a bad idea when you're checking out a project from multiple places in a repository; files move in relation to one another, and the build becomes tricky to orchestrate.

However, when subprojects don't depend on each other, this kind of renaming can be a great convenience. For example, at the Pragmatic Programmers offices we keep all our work in a central CVS repository. It contains project code, documentation, our websites, and the sources to our books. Much of this stuff is independent; the course material for *Introduction to Ruby* doesn't depend on anything else in the repository, so it makes sense to be able to check it out on its own. So in our own modules file, you'll find the lines

```
courses  PP/doc/Courses
halfruby PP/doc/Courses/HalfDayRuby
```

This means that we can check out the module `halfruby` and the course material will appear in a directory of the same name; there's no need to create (or traverse) a full directory tree to get to this single set of files. Note also that the alias doesn't have to point to a leaf directory; checking out the module courses will fetch all our course material.

Alias modules let us put multiple directories and other aliases in the module definition. We can't do this with regular modules; each definition must reference exactly one directory (but see the next section on ampersand modules for a way around this). However, you can perform one extra piece of magic with regular modules; you can include a list of specific files and directories after the main directory path. If you do this, only those files and directories will be checked out.

For example, the files in the Half-Day Ruby course are pretty large. If I was in a hotel room using a dial-up connection and I needed just the sample code for the course, I wouldn't want to waste time downloading megabytes worth of Powerpoint presentations. I could check out just the samples subdirectory using a CVS command; CVS is smart enough to let you add paths to modules just as you can with top-level directories.

```
work> cvs co halfruby/samples
```

However, if this was something that we did a lot, we could add a line to the modules file.

```
halfrubysamp PP/doc/Courses/HalfDayRuby/samples
```

Checking out the module halfrubysamp will create a directory called halfrubysamp and populate it with the samples from the repository.

Ampersand Modules

Earlier we said that in general, modules can be rooted in only a single directory. However, that was a wee lie. There's an additional syntax that can be used to overcome that restriction. A module may be defined in terms of a list of other modules by prefixing those other modules' name with an ampersand character ("&"). For example, Andy and Dave may have modules set up for all their Ruby courses and talks.

```
halfruby   PP/doc/Courses/HalfDayRuby
fullruby   PP/doc/Courses/OneDayRuby
introruby  PP/doc/Talks/IntroRuby
vacation   PP/doc/Talks/SummerVacation
   :          :
```

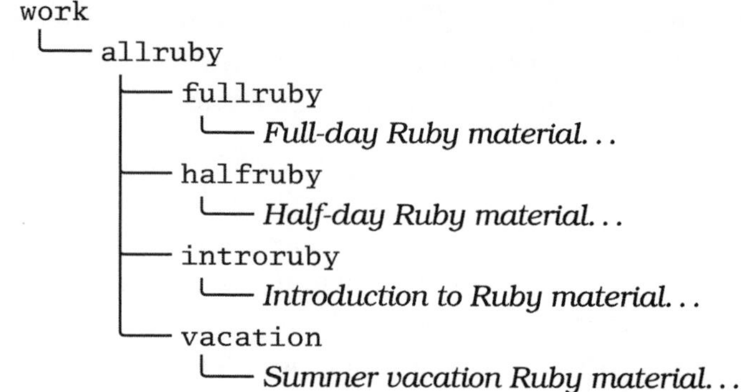

Figure 9.5: CHECKING-OUT AN AMPERSAND MODULE

It would be convenient to be able to check all of these out with a single command. We could do this by adding a new module.

```
allruby   &halfruby &fullruby &introruby &vacation . . .
```

We could then check out all our Ruby material using a single command.

```
work> cvs co allruby
```

This checks out the Ruby material into the directory structure shown in Figure 9.5. The top-level directory is named after the module, and its immediate children are named after the included modules.

We could also have used this approach to tidy up the alias for `halfrubysamp` on the page before.

```
halfrubysamp &halfruby/samples
```

9.3 Summary

Use CVS modules when you want to create a logical structure for your project by bringing together separate pieces from your repository. They reduce developer error by giving you a single place to define exactly what is meant by a particular project or subproject. They also allow you to maintain a consistent external structure for all your projects.

Chapter 10

Third-Party Code

All projects rely to some extent on external libraries: C programs use the `libc` library, Java programs use `rt.jar`, and so on. Should these libraries form part of your personal workspace?

To answer that question, ask yourself another. You need to be able to rebuild a working program at some arbitrary time in the future. Will you be able to use the versions of these libraries that will be available then?

If you feel comfortable that the libraries used by your code will be available (and compatible) over the life of your application, then there's no need to do anything special with them; just use them as installed on your machine.

Looking beyond standard language facilities, many projects include other, less stable, libraries in their projects. For example, many Java developers will use the JUnit framework[1] to test their code. Compared to the standard libraries, these frameworks are fairly volatile (as of June 2003, JUnit is already up to version 3.8). Although the changes between versions are mostly compatible, there can be changes that affect your application.[2] As a result, we'd recommend that you

---

[1] `http://www.junit.org`

[2] For example, we've seen interactions between the Ant build tool and various revisions of JUnit.

include these libraries in your workspace, and (by extension) in your project's repositories.

Having made the decision that you want to include a third party library in your workspace and repository, you now have to decide what to include and where to put it.

The first decision is what files to include. This is relatively easy. If you use the library in the form distributed by the maker, and you feel confident that the library will continue to work unmodified through the life of the application, then storing the binary form of the library is all that is needed. We suggest putting all these libraries in subdirectories of a top-level `vendor/` directory. If the library is architecture-independent (for example a Java `.jar` file), then it can simply sit in a subdirectory called `lib/`. If instead you have libraries that depend on the target architecture (and assuming your application is targeted at more than one architecture) you'll need to have subdirectories below `vendor/` for each architecture and operating system combination. A common naming scheme for these subdirectories is to use *arch-os* where *arch* is the target architecture (i586 for an Intel Pentium, ppc for a PowerPC, and so on) and *os* is the operating system (linux, win2k, and so on). Always remember to use the `-kb` flag when importing or adding a binary file (such as a .DLL (dynamic link library) or other library) to CVS.

Languages such as C and C++ require that you include source header files in application code that uses a particular library. These header files are supplied with the library, and should also be stored in the workspace and repository. We suggest storing them in an `include/` subdirectory beneath `vendor`. Structure the subdirectories of `vendor/include/` in such a way that the compilers can find the libraries' include files naturally. As an example, consider a C library called `datetime` which performs date and time calculations. It comes with a binary library archive, `libdatetime.a`, and two header files, `datetime.h` and `extras.h`. The `datetime.h` header library is intended to be installed at the top level of the include hierarchy, while `extras.h` is expected to be in a subdirectory called `dt/`. That is, a program that used both header files would normally start:

```
proj/                ← top level of project
└── vendor/
    ├── lib/
    │   └── libdatetime.a
    └── include/
        ├── datetime.h
        └── dt/
            └── extras.h
```

Figure 10.1: SAMPLE REPOSITORY WITH THIRD PARTY LIBRARY

```
#include <datetime>
#include <dt/extras>
// . . .
```

In this case, we'd organize our repository (and our workspace) as shown in Figure 10.1.

Integrating with the Build Environment

If you include vendor libraries or header files in your workspace, you'll need to make sure that your compilers, linkers, and IDEs can get to them. There's a minor problem: you need to make sure that you don't check anything in to the repository that contains absolute path names (as this might not work on some other developer's machine). Instead, you have a couple of options:

1. Arrange your build tools so that all path names are relative to (say) the top level project directory. This is workable if you're using an external build tool such as "make" or "ant," but it can get tricky.

2. Set up some external environment variable to point to the top of the project tree, and make all references in the build relative to this variable. This allows each developer to have different values in the external variable, but then to share a common build environment layout.

   The external variable need not be a true operating system environment variable. The Eclipse IDE, for example, allows each user to set internal variables, and then to have a common shared build structure that references these variables. This means that all developers can share a common Eclipse build definition, but that developers can still install the source in different locations.

We recommend the second approach.

10.1 Libraries With Source Code

Sometimes a library comes with source code (or is distributed only as source code). If you have both source and binary versions of the library available, which should you store in the repository, and how should you set up your workspace?

The answer is an exercise in risk management. Having the source available means that you are always in the position (technically, at least) to fix bugs and add features, something you can't do with a binary library. This is clearly a good thing. At the same time, including the source code for all the libraries used by your project can slow down builds and complicate the structure of your project. It also gives future maintainers a headache. If there's a bug, do they need to consider potential changes to the library source, or can they concentrate on the code written by your organization?

Our recommendation is to add vendor source to your repository, but to treat it specially. To do this, you have to do a bit of role-playing.

Imagine for a minute that you are the writer of this particular library, and that every now and then you release an updated version of the code to your user base. Being a high-quality library writer, you naturally put all your source in a version control system, and practice all the necessary release control procedures.

Now come back from the role-play (remember, breathe in, breathe out, breathe in, breathe out). In an ideal world, we should be able to hook straight in to our vendor's repository and extract releases directly from there. But we can't, so we have to do the work ourselves. Whenever we receive code, bug fixes, and new releases from a vendor, we have to pretend that *we* had generated the code, and handle it in our version control system as if we were the vendor handling it in theirs. This turns out to be simpler than it sounds.

Importing the Initial Source

When we first receive the source code for a third-party library, we need to import it into our repository. We recommend keeping this code separate from the code of your project. If you anticipate importing code from multiple sources over time, it probably makes sense to keep it all under a common top-level directory; we suggest calling it `vendorsrc/` (to differentiate it from `vendor/`, which contains libraries and header files).

To make this more concrete, let's assume that we've decided to use version 4.3 of the GNU readline library in our project (after checking the license terms, of course).

We start by downloading the latest sources from the GNU ftp site. We'll store this in a temporary directory.

```
~> cd tmp
tmp> ftp ftp.gnu.org
Connected to ftp.gnu.org.
Name (ftp.gnu.org:dave): ftp
331 Please specify the password.
Password:
230 Login successful. Have fun.
Using binary mode to transfer files.
ftp> cd pub/gnu/readline
250 Directory successfully changed.
ftp> get readline-4.3.tar.gz
local: readline-4.3.tar.gz remote: readline-4.3.tar.gz
961662 bytes received in 00:06 (136.48 KB/s)
ftp> bye
221 Goodbye.
```

We then unpack the archive. This creates a source tree in a subdirectory (which we know from experience will be called `readline-4.3`). We make this our current working directory.

```
tmp> tar zxf readline-4.3.tar.gz
tmp> cd readline-4.3
```

We are now in a position to import this source into our repository. We'll store it in the repository under `vendorsrc/fsf/readline`. (Remember, all our third-party code is stored under `vendorsrc/`. In this case, the vendor is the Free Software Foundation, and the "product" is readline.)

```
tmp/readline-4.3>  cvs import -ko -I! -m "load 4.3" \
                       vendorsrc/fsf/readline FSF_RL RL_4_3
N import/aclocal.m4
N import/ansi_stdlib.h
N import/bind.c
N import/callback.c
    :      :
N import/support/shobj-conf
N import/support/wcwidth.c
No conflicts created by this import
```

-ko ⇒ *Keywords Off*

That's quite a command: we break it down in Figure 10.2 on the next page. The -ko flag is important, but subtle. Normally, CVS will expand special keywords (such as $Author$) in each of the files it manages. This lets you add annotations to the files. (This isn't a practice we encourage, so we haven't shown it so far in this book.) The problem is that the keywords are expanded every time the file is checked out. If the vendor also uses CVS, and if the vendor has used these tags, then the source you receive will have the vendor's information in these fields. However, if you just import these files as they stand and check them back out, CVS will update the tags, and suddenly your name will appear in the author field. While this may be vaguely satisfying, it will cause problems later when you come to merge in changes with the next vendor release. CVS will notice that these tag lines have changed, and you'll get conflicts when merging with the vendor's code. Specifying the -ko option turns off tag expansion for all files in the import, so you won't see this problem.

-I! ⇒ *Ignore Nothing!*

The -I! is equally subtle; it tells CVS not to ignore any files while importing. When you're working with your own directories, you'll probably want CVS to bypass processing of backup files and the like, but with vendor-supplied files, you're going to want to load everything into the repository.

The *vendor tag* gives us a way to name the product we're importing. In this case, all the code for readline can be referenced using the tag FSF_RL. The *release tag* specifies the code that makes up this particular release. If the FSF comes up with version 4.4 of readline, we'll check it in with a different release tag. This means that we'll always be able to get back to the 4.3 release using the original RL_4_3 tag.

Having imported this code into the repository, we can delete the temporary directory that we used.

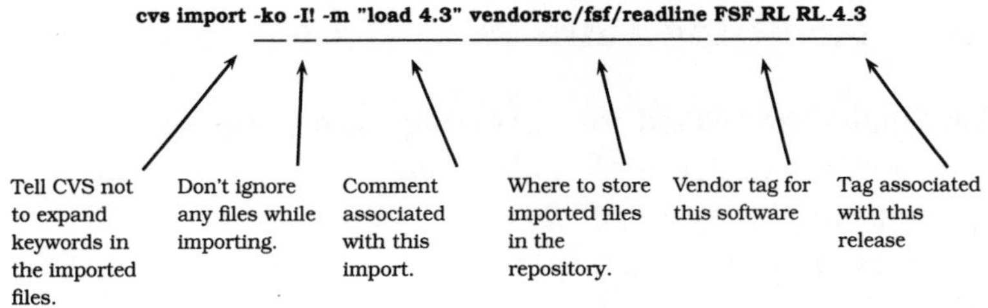
cvs import -ko -I! -m "load 4.3" vendorsrc/fsf/readline FSF_RL RL_4_3
Tell CVS not to expand keywords in the imported files.
Don't ignore any files while importing.
Comment associated with this import.
Where to store imported files in the repository.
Vendor tag for this software
Tag associated with this release

Figure 10.2: A CVS "IMPORT" COMMAND

Importing New Vendor Releases

When a vendor releases a new version of their software, you might want to incorporate it into your repository.[3] Assuming that you haven't made any local changes to the vendor's source code, then this is easy; simply import it again, following the same steps as above:

1. Download the new source, and unpack it in to a temporary directory.
2. Issue a CVS import command, using the same repository location and vendor tag, but with an updated release tag.

For example, if the FSF released readline version 4.4, we could do:

```
tmp>  tar zxf readline-4.4.tar.gz
tmp>  cd readline-4.4
tmp/readline-4.4>  cvs import -m -ko -I! "load 4.4" \
                           vendorsrc/fsf/readline FSF_RL RL_4_4
N import/aclocal.m4
N import/ansi_stdlib.h
N import/bind.c
N import/callback.c
N import/chardefs.h
N import/compat.c
    :      :
N import/support/shobj-conf
N import/support/wcwidth.c
No conflicts created by this import
```

[3]Many teams make the mistake of constantly chasing the latest and greatest vendor releases. This isn't always prudent. If the features added at a particular release don't enhance your application, is it worth the risk of incorporating new code? Sometimes skipping minor releases and only merging major changes is a better idea.

10.2 Modifying Third-Party Code

Sometimes the reason for importing third-party source code is to allow your team to make changes. You may need to add some application-specific functionality, or you might have local bug fixes that you need to apply.

Clearly the ideal solution would be to supply this changed code back to the third party and let them incorporate it into their own copy. That way when they send you the next release, their code will incorporate your changes, and life will be wonderful.

However, that isn't always possible. In these cases, we need to maintain our local changes and (ideally) have them automatically roll forward from each vendor release to the next.

Fortunately for us, CVS makes this relatively easy. In the background, the import mechanism is actually building and managing a simple release tree. It works like this.

When you first import code into CVS, it creates a mainline, and then immediately creates a branch (numbered 1.1.1). It then places the code that you import into this branch (so the first source files will have a revision number of 1.1.1.1). Although this sounds complicated, it's really no different to the description we had of a simple release structure back on page 18. And that isn't a coincidence; behind the scenes CVS is handing these imports as if you were the vendor performing releases. The vendor tag that you give the import command turns out to be the tag given to the release branch, and the release tags given on each import identify the points on that branch where each individual release's code sits. This is illustrated in Figure 10.3 on the next page.

If you check out vendor code, you'll be checking out of the release branch (the branch labeled with the vendor tag). You can verify this; doing a `cvs status` on a file will show a revision number with four levels (so the first revision will be 1.1.1.1). However, there's some magic here. If you edit vendor code and check it back in, CVS will place your changes in the mainline, but the revision number will be 1.2, not 1.1.1.2. CVS reserves the code in the vendor branch for vendor code.

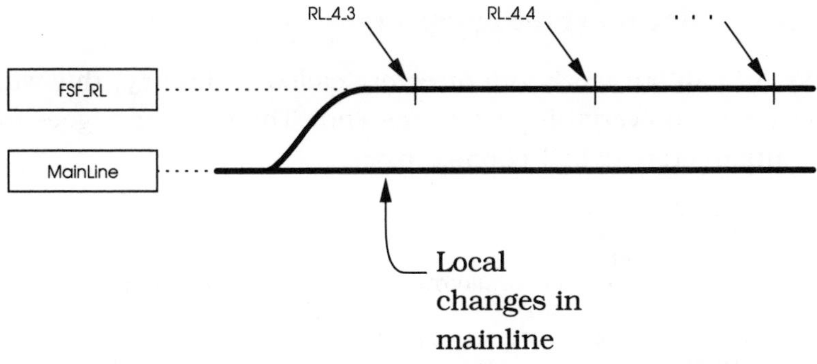

Figure 10.3: IMPORTED THIRD PARTY CODE. CODE IS IMPORTED IN TO A RELEASE BRANCH, LABELED BY THE VENDOR TAG. EACH IMPORT GENERATES A NEW RELEASE TAG IN THAT BRANCH. LOCAL WORK AUTOMATICALLY TAKES PLACE IN THE MAINLINE.

What happens if you edit third-party code, and then a new release comes along? Let's find out. To do this, we'll set up a dummy repository. We'll then pretend to be a vendor (called Acme) and create a couple of simple files. With our project team hat back on, we'll then import these, and check them out into our workspace. We'll then make a change and check it in.

Back in the vendor directory we'll prepare an updated release. We'll then try to import it, and we'll work out how to merge the vendor changes with our own.

Because all this role playing can get confusing, once we get started we'll show the full path of the current directory at the start of each of the sequences of commands. In the prompts themselves, we'll just show the directory name. In general, when we're playing vendor we'll be in the directory:

```
tmp/3rdparty/Acme
```

When we're a client dealing with checked-out vendor files we'll be in the directory:

```
tmp/3rdparty/work/vendorsrc/Acme
```

Step 1: Set up the Repository

We'll do all our work in a directory called `3rdparty`; this will let us clean everything up at the end. The repository goes in a subdirectory called `repository`.

```
# In directory tmp
tmp>  mkdir 3rdparty
tmp>  cd 3rdparty
tmp/3rdparty>  export CVSROOT=~/tmp/3rdparty/repository
tmp/3rdparty>  cvs init
tmp/3rdparty>  ls     # use 'dir' under Windows
repository
```

Step 2: Create the Third-Party Code

We'll create a directory called Acme that contains the third-party code. This directory will be the one we import into CVS. We'll use an editor to create two files, `Color.txt` and `Number.txt` using our favorite editor.

```
# in directory tmp/3rdparty
tmp/3rdparty>  mkdir Acme
tmp/3rdparty>  cd Acme
```

edit files, giving...

File `Color.txt`:

```
black
brown
red
orange
yellow
green
```

File `Number.txt`:

```
zero
one
two
three
four
```

Step 3: Import the Vendor Code

We've finished playing vendor for a minute. Now we'll pretend that we've received this code from the vendor and import it in to the repository, storing it in `vendorsrc/Acme`.

```
# In directory tmp/3rdparty/Acme
Acme>  cvs import -ko -m "load" vendorsrc/Acme Acme REL_1_0
N vendorsrc/Acme/Color.txt
N vendorsrc/Acme/Number.txt
No conflicts created by this import
```

Step 4: Set Up The Workspace

We'll now create a workspace and check out this vendor code there.

```
# In directory tmp/3rdparty/Acme
Acme>  cd ..
tmp/3rdparty>  mkdir work
tmp/3rdparty>  cd work
tmp/3rdparty/work>  cvs co vendorsrc/Acme
cvs checkout: Updating vendorsrc/Acme
U vendorsrc/Acme/Color.txt
U vendorsrc/Acme/Number.txt
```

Step 5: Modify The Vendor Code

Part way through our project, we discover a problem in the vendor code; their numbers file uses "zero," but our project standards call for "naught." The vendor ignores our pleas for a change, claiming we are their only customer to use Middle-English numbering (can that be?). So we bite the bullet and make the change ourselves. We edit the file in our workspace, then check it back in.

```
# In directory tmp/3rdparty/work
work>  cd vendorsrc/Acme
Acme>  # ... edit file ...
Acme>  cvs commit -m "Zero becomes naught"
cvs commit: Examining .
Checking in Number.txt;
.../repository/vendorsrc/Acme/Number.txt,v  <--  Number.txt
new revision: 1.2; previous revision: 1.1
done
```

Step 6: The Vendor Makes a Change

Meanwhile, back at Acme Corp, they decide to produce V1.1 of the product. As part of the added value in this new release, they're adding three new numbers to their numbers file. We'll simulate this by going back to our Acme directory (the one at the top level) and editing the file.

```
# In directory tmp/3rdparty/work/vendorsrc/Acme
Acme>  cd ../../../Acme
tmp/3rdparty/Acme>  # ... edit file ...
```

After the edit, the new numbers file contains:

File Number.txt:

```
zero
one
two
three
four
five
six
seven
```

This file still has "zero" in it; remember that Acme did not make the change to "naught." That's only in our local copy.

Step 7: Import the New Revision

Acme sends us the new revision, so with our client hats on we import it into CVS.

```
# In directory tmp/3rdparty/Acme
Acme>  cvs import -ko -I! -m "update" vendorsrc/Acme Acme REL_1_1
U vendorsrc/Acme/Color.txt
C vendorsrc/Acme/Number.txt
1 conflicts created by this import.
Use the following command to help the merge:
        cvs checkout -jAcme:yesterday -jAcme vendorsrc/Acme
```

CVS was smart enough to recognize that this import was actually updating existing files. The Color.txt file updated successfully (in fact it is unchanged) but the Number.txt file has a potential conflict; it has been changed by us (as the client) and also by the vendor. CVS was nice enough to suggest the command we could use to fix the situation. Normally, this command would work fine. Unfortunately it won't work for us. To see why, let's look at the command in more detail.

As we saw in Chapter 7.2, the -j option is used to merge in changes during checkout or update. In this case we're using two -j options. The first option, -jAcme:yesterday, tells CVS to look at the Acme branch as it was yesterday, before (in theory) we imported the latest release. The second, -jAcme says look at it as it is now. The two together ask CVS to compute the difference; this difference is the changes that the vendor made. These changes are then applied to the current head of our mainline. The net result of all this is that the vendor's changes are used to update our local copy.

Although this incantation would normally work (because few vendors produce more than one release per day), it doesn't work too well in our example, as we didn't even have any vendor code yesterday. Instead, we'll use an alternate form of the -j option, which allows us to merge based on release tags.

To do this, change back to our workspace, and issue the following command.

```
# In directory tmp/3rdparty/Acme
Acme>  cd ../work
work>  cvs co -jREL_1_0 -jREL_1_1 vendorsrc/Acme
cvs checkout: Updating vendorsrc/Acme
RCS file: /Users/dave/tmp/3rdparty/repository/vendorsrc/Acme/Number.txt,v
retrieving revision 1.1.1.1
retrieving revision 1.1.1.2
Merging differences between 1.1.1.1 and 1.1.1.2 into Number.txt
```

Remember that we gave the first import the revision tag of REL_1_0 and the second the tag REL_1_1. This lets us tell CVS to apply the differences between these two releases to our current mainline code. The result can be seen in the tracing that follows the command: CVS merges the vendor's changes in to our local file. Let's look at it and confirm that we have the vendor's three additional numbers, and that our "naught" has not been changed.

```
# In directory tmp/3rdparty/work
work>  cd vendorsrc/Acme
Acme>  cvs status Number.txt
===================================================================
File: Number.txt           Status: Locally Modified

   Working revision:    1.2       Result of merge
   Repository revision: 1.2       /Users/dave/tmp/3rdparty/repos...
   Sticky Tag:          (none)
   Sticky Date:         (none)
   Sticky Options:      (none)
```

We can also check the file contents.

File `Number.txt`:

```
naught
one
two
three
four
five
six
seven
```

Had there been conflicts between the vendor code and our changes, we'd have seen the normal conflict markers in the file.

Step 8: Save the Merged File

Now that we've merged the changes (and run the tests to confirm the system still works) we can check everything back in to the repository.

```
# In directory tmp/3rdparty/work/vendorsrc/Acme
Acme>  cvs commit -m "Merged 1.1 changes"
cvs commit: Examining .
Checking in Number.txt;
/Users/.../vendorsrc/Acme/Number.txt,v  <--  Number.txt
new revision: 1.3; previous revision: 1.2
done
```

Summary: Modifying Third-Party Code

Managing vendor releases using these simple steps is both straightforward and powerful. CVS automatically maintains a release branch that contains the unmodified code from the vendor, tagged at each release. Our mainline in the repository contains the same code, but with all our local changes. Using the `-j` options allows us to merge the vendor's changes at each release into our local version of their code.

To summarize, the steps are:

- Import the vendor code:

```
cvs import -ko -I! -m "load" \
           vendor_module vendor release_tag
```

- Check out vendor code into a local workspace:

```
cd work
cvs co vendor_module
```

- Make local changes to vendor code and check back in:

```
cvs commit -m "summary of changes"
```

- If the vendor issues a new release, import it into the vendor branch:

```
cvs import -ko -I! -m "update" \
           vendor_module vendor release_tag
```

- Fix conflicts between vendor changes and our changes:

```
cvs co -jrelease_1 -jrelease_2 vendor_module
```

- Save the changes back:

```
cvs commit -m "summary of changes"
```

Appendix A

CVS Summary and Recipes

This section is a brief summary of CVS commands, and the particular recipes used in this book.

A.1 CVS Command Format

cvs <*global options..*> *command* <*options and arguments...*>

Global Options	
-H	Displays usage information for command.
-Q	Cause CVS to be really quiet.
-q	Cause CVS to be somewhat quiet.
-r	Make checked-out files read-only.
-w	Make checked-out files read-write (default).
-l	Turn history logging off.
-n	Do not execute anything that will change the disk.
-t	Show trace of program execution – try with -n.
-v	CVS version and copyright.
-b *bindir*	Find RCS programs in "bindir".
-T *tmpdir*	Use "tmpdir" for temporary files.
-e *editor*	Use "editor" for editing log information.
-d *CVSROOT*	Overrides CVSROOT environment variable as the root of the CVS tree.
-f	Do not use the /.cvsrc file.
-z #	Use compression level "#" for net traffic.
-a	Authenticate all net traffic.
-s *VAR=VAL*	Set CVS user variable.

Flag Characters

During update operations, CVS will display a list of file names preceded by flag characters. The following table lists the meanings of these characters.

A *file* — *file* has been added locally and is not yet in the repository.

C *file* — A conflict was detected when trying to update *file* (that is, local changes conflicted with changes made in the repository version). Your local copy of the file contains conflict markers, and the original version of the file is stored in a new file called `.#file.version`.

M *file* — *file* has been modified in your workspace and needs to be stored back to bring the repository up-to-date.

P *file* — Equivalent to "U," documented below. The "P" flag signifies that the server used a patch to bring the file up to date.

R *file* — *file* has been removed from your working copy of the repository (using `cvs remove`). The repository version will be removed when you run `cvs commit`.

U *file* — The local copy of *file* has been updated to bring it up-to-date with the repository. This happens both when the repository version is later than the local version and when a new file is in the repository but not (yet) available locally.

? *file* — *file* exists in your workspace but nothing is known about it in the repository. You can use `cvs add` to add it, or possibly update `.cvsignore` to tell CVS to ignore it.

CVS Environment

The following environment variables are commonly used with CVS. They are described in more detail in *Connecting to CVS* on page 51.

CVSROOT

Specifies the default repository location and access method. Setting this variable means you don't need to use the global CVS `-d` option.

CVS_RSH

Specifies the program to be used to access the remote repository. We recommend using `ssh` for this purpose.

CVS Commands

CVS supports a rich set of commands, listed in the table that follows. In this book we use only a subset of these (marked † in the following table). In the sections that follow, we'll show the specific options for these commands. These descriptions are based on the CVS help information: use `cvs --help` for details.

add†	Add a new file/directory to the repository
admin†	Administration front end for rcs
annotate†	Show last revision where each line was modified
checkout†	Checkout sources for editing
commit†	Check files into the repository
diff†	Show differences between revisions
edit	Get ready to edit a watched file
editors	See who is editing a watched file
export	Export sources from CVS, similar to checkout
history	Show repository access history
import†	Import sources into CVS, using vendor branches
init†	Create a CVS repository if it doesn't exist
log†	Print out history information for files
login†	Prompt for password for authenticating server
logout†	Removes entry in .cvspass for remote repository
rdiff	Create "patch" format diffs between releases
release†	Indicate that a module is no longer in use
remove†	Remove an entry from the repository
rtag†	Add a symbolic tag to a module
status†	Display status information on checked out files
tag†	Add a symbolic tag to checked out version of files
unedit	Undo an edit command
update†	Bring work tree in sync with repository
watch	Set watches
watchers	See who is watching a file

add

Add New File or Directory

```
cvs add  [-k rcs-kflag] [-m message] files...
```

-k Use *rcs-kflag* to add the file with the specified kflag. Commonly used as "-kb" to add binary files to the repository.

-m Use *message* for the creation log.

admin

Administer Underlying Repository

```
cvs admin  rcsoptions...
```

-k Use "rcs-kflag" to change the flags associated with a file. Sometimes used to change the status of a file to binary (using "-kb").

annotate

Show Revisions for Lines in Files

```
cvs annotate  [-lRf] [-r rev|-D date] [files...]
```

-l	Local directory only, no recursion.
-R	Process directories recursively.
-f	Use head revision if tag/date not found.
-r *rev*	Annotate file as of specified revision/tag.
-D *date*	Annotate file as of specified date.

Check Out Sources For Editing `checkout`

```
cvs checkout  [-ANPRcflnps] [-r rev| -D date]
              [-d dir] [-j rev1] [-j rev2] [-k kopt]
              modules...
```

-A	Reset any sticky tags/date/kopts.
-N	Don't shorten module paths if -d specified.
-P	Prune empty directories.
-R	Process directories recursively.
-c	Show contents of the module database.
-f	Force a head revision match if tag/date not found.
-l	Local directory only, not recursive.
-n	Do not run module program (if any).
-p	Check out files to standard output (avoids stickiness).
-s	Like -c, but include module status.
-r *rev*	Check out revision or tag (implies -P; is sticky).
-D *date*	Check out revisions as of date (implies -P; is sticky).
-d *dir*	Check out into dir instead of module name.
-k *kopt*	Use RCS kopt -k option on checkout.
-j *rev*	Merge in changes made between current revision and rev.

Check Files in to the Repository `commit`

```
cvs commit  [-nRlf] [-m msg | -F logfile] [-r rev]
            files...
```

-n	Do not run the module program (if any).
-R	Process directories recursively.
-l	Local directory only (not recursive).
-f	Force the file to be committed; disables recursion.
-F *file*	Read the log message from file.
-m *msg*	Log message.
-r *rev*	Commit to this branch or trunk revision.

diff

Show Differences Between Revisions

```
cvs diff  [-lNR] [rcsdiff-options]
          [[-r rev1 | -D date1] [-r rev2 | -D date2]]
          [files...]
```

-l	Local directory only, not recursive.
-R	Process directories recursively.
-D *date1*	Diff revision for date against working file.
-D *date2*	Diff rev1/date1 against date2.
-N	Include diffs for added and removed files.
-r *rev1*	Diff revision for rev1 against working file.
-r *rev2*	Diff rev1/date1 against rev2.
–ifdef=*arg*	Output diffs in ifdef format.
rcsdiff	Common options include `-c` for context diffs, `-u` for unified diffs, and `--side-by-side`.

import

Import Sources Into CVS

```
cvs import  [-d] [-k subst] [-I ign] [-m msg]
            [-b branch] [-W spec] repository
            vendor-tag release-tags...
```

-d	Use the file's modification time as the time of import.
-k *sub*	Set default RCS keyword substitution mode.
-I *ign*	Files to ignore (! to reset).
-b *bra*	Vendor branch id.
-m *msg*	Log message.
-W *spec*	Wrappers specification line.

init

Create a CVS Repository

```
cvs init
```

Print File History — `log`

```
cvs log  [-lRhtNb] [-r[revisions]] [-d dates]
         [-s states] [-w[logins]] [files...]
```

-l — Local directory only, no recursion.
-R — Only print name of RCS file.
-h — Only print header.
-t — Only print header and descriptive text.
-N — Do not list tags.
-b — Only list revisions on the default branch.
-r[*revisions*] — Specify revision(s)s to list.
-d *dates* — Specify dates (D1<D2 for range, D for latest before).
-s *states* — Only list revisions with specified states.
-w[*logins*] — Only list revisions checked in by specified logins.

Log In to PServer — `login`

```
cvs login
```

Stop Using a Module — `release`

```
cvs release  [-d] directories...
```

-d — Delete the local copy of the given directories.

Remove Entry from Repository — `remove`

```
cvs remove  [-flR] [files...]
```

-f — Delete the file before removing it.
-l — Process this directory only (not recursive).
-R — Process directories recursively.

rtag

Tag Module in Repository

```
cvs rtag  [-aflRnF] [-b] [-d] [-r tag|-D date] tag
          modules...
```

-a	Clear tag from removed files that would not otherwise be tagged.
-f	Force a head revision match if tag/date not found.
-l	Local directory only, not recursive.
-R	Process directories recursively.
-n	No execution of "tag program".
-d	Delete the given tag.
-b	Make the tag a "branch" tag, allowing concurrent development.
-r *rev*	Existing revision/tag.
-D	Existing date.
-F	Move tag if it already exists.

status

Display Status of Files

```
cvs status  [-vlR] [files...]
```

-v	Verbose format; includes tag information for the file.
-l	Process this directory only (not recursive).
-R	Process directories recursively.

tag

Tag Local Files

```
cvs tag  [-lRF] [-b] [-d] [-c] [-r tag |-D date] tag
         [files...]
```

-l	Local directory only, not recursive.
-R	Process directories recursively.
-d	Delete the given tag.
-r *rev*	Existing revision/tag.
-D *date*	Existing date.
-f	Force a head revision if specified tag not found.
-b	Make the tag a "branch" tag, allowing concurrent development.
-F	Move tag if it already exists.
-c	Check that working files are unmodified.

Bring Local Files Up To Date

`update`

```
cvs update  [-APdflRp] [-k kopt] [-r rev |-D date]
            [-j rev] [-I ign] [-W spec] [files...]
```

-A	Reset any sticky tags/date/kopts.
-P	Prune empty directories.
-d	Build directories, like checkout does.
-f	Force a head revision match if tag/date not found.
-l	Local directory only, no recursion.
-R	Process directories recursively.
-p	Send updates to standard output (avoids stickiness).
-k *kopt*	Use RCS kopt -k option on checkout.
-r *rev*	Update using specified revision/tag (is sticky).
-D *date*	Set date to update from (is sticky).
-j *rev*	Merge in changes made between current revision and rev.
-I *ign*	Files to ignore (! to reset).
-W *spec*	Wrappers specification line.

A.2 Recipes

Connecting via SSH .... *Page 56*

set CVSROOT to :ext:*user@address*:*repository*

set CVS_RSH to ssh

Issue normal CVS commands.

Connecting via pserver .... *Page 57*

set CVSROOT to :pserver:*user@address*:*repository*

cvs login

Checking things out .... *Page 60*

cvs co *module*...

Checking out a particular revision .... *Page 60*

cvs co -r *tag module*

Updating a Workspace .... *Page 62*

cvs -q update -d

Updating Specific Files .... *Page 62*

cvs -q update *file*...

Adding Files and Directories .... *Page 65*

cvs add *name*...

Adding Binary Files .... *Page 65*

cvs add -kb *name*...

Ignoring certain files .... *Page 70*

Add names to .cvsignore file

(remember to cvs add .cvsignore)

Renaming files .... *Page 71*

cvs -q update -d

rename old_name to new_name

cvs remove *old_name*

cvs add *new_name*

cvs commit -m "Rename *old_name* to *new_name*"

Renaming a Directory .... *Page 73*

mkdir *new_dir*

cvs add *new_dir*

move files from old_dir/ new_dir...

cvs remove *old_dir/file*...

cvs add *new_dir/file*...

cvs commit -m "Rename *old_dir/* to *new_dir/*"

cvs update -P

Seeing what's changed since checkout .... *Page 74*

cvs diff *file or dir*

Seeing what's changed between versions .... *Page 75*

cvs diff -r *r1* [-r *r2*] *file or dir*

Committing changes .... Page 82

```
cvs commit -m "message"
```

Examining change history .... Page 83

```
cvs log file or dir
cvs annotate file or dir
```

Undo change made between r1 and r2 .... Page 87

```
cvs update -jr2 -jr1 file
```

Checking Workspace Status .... Page 89

```
cvs -nq update -d
#  ... or ...
alias cvstat="cvs status 2>&1     |
               egrep '(\?|File:)' |
               grep -v Up-to-date"
```

Creating a Release Branch .... Page 95

```
cvs commit -m "..."
cvs rtag -b RB_x_y project
```

Checking out a Release Branch .... Page 96

```
cd work
cvs co -r RB_x_y -d rbx.y project
```

Generating a Release .... Page 97

```
cvs update
# ... run tests ...
cvs commit -m "..."  # if needed
cvs tag REL_x_y
```

Checking Out a Release .... Page 97

```
cd work
cvs co -r REL_x_y -d relx.y project
```

Fixing Bugs in a Release Branch .... Page 99

```
cd work
cvs co -r RB_x_y -d rbx.y project
cd rbx.y
cvs tag PRE_bugno
# create test, fix problem, validate
cvs commit -m "Fix PRbugno"
cvs tag POST_bugno
```

Apply Bug Fix to Another Branch .... Page 100

```
cd workingdir
cvs update
cvs -j PRE_bugno -j POST_bugno update
# test...
cvs commit -m "Apply fix for PRbugno from RBx.y"
```

Creating Experimental Branches .... Page 100

```
cvs commit -m ""
cvs rtag -b TRY_initials_yymmdd project
```

```
cvs update -r TRY_initials_yymmdd
```



```
cvs update -A
```


In experimental workspace:

```
cvs commit -m "Finalize changes"
cd mainline
cvs update -j TRY_initials_yymmdd
```



```
cvs co CVSROOT
cd CVSROOT
edit file: modules
cvs commit -m "Add module name"
cd ..
cvs release -d CVSROOT
```



```
cvs import -ko -I! -m "msg" rep_locn vendor tag
```

Appendix B

Other Resources

CVS is probably the most commonly used version control system in the world, so help is normally just a Google query away. However, here are some resources that we find especially useful.

B.1 Online CVS Resources

CVS Home Page
⇒ `www.cvshome.org`
The canonical site for CVS. Here you'll find information on new releases, downloads, the list of Frequently Asked Questions, and documentation.

Clicking the *Hosted Projects* link in the side panel takes you to a list of auxiliary CVS projects. Under the *Integration* link you'll find tools that might help you integrate CVS with your particular environment.

CVS Manual
⇒ `www.cvshome.org/docs/manual/`
Per Cederqvist's manual for CVS is available in HTML, PDF, and Postscript formats.

B.2 Other CVS Books

This book takes a recipe-based approach to CVS. We believe that the commands documented here represent the essential subset of CVS for the vast majority of project teams. The bibliography contains references to three other CVS books

([Fog99], [Pur00], and [Ves03]) which contain more detailed information on the nitty-gritty of CVS.

It also contains a reference to a higher-level book, Software Configuration Management Patterns [BA03], which explains some of the theory behind the things we do with version control systems.

B.3 Other Version Control Systems

The list below is a set of pointers to some well-known version control systems. We've tried hard to be non-judgemental; different folks are looking for different capabilities in their tools. Before investing in any of the commercial products, we strongly recommend searching for other users and getting their opinions. You'll find some surprisingly strong reactions. . . .

BitKeeper
⇒ `www.bitkeeper.com`
BitKeeper uses an interesting approach to version control; it operates largely without a central server or repository.

ClearCase
⇒ `www.rational.com/products/clearcase/index.jsp`
Originally a Rational product, now owned by IBM.

Forte Code Management Software
⇒ `wwws.sun.com/software/sundev/previous/teamware`
Formerly by Forte TeamWare, now owned by Sun, and the inspiration for BitKeeper.

PVCS
⇒ `www.merant.com`
The professional offering includes version control, change management, bug tracking, and build automation.

Perforce
⇒ `www.perforce.com`
Powerful version control system. Many developers feel it has the simplest-to-use branching model.

Subversion
⇒ `subversion.tigris.org`
An open-source project intended to produce an eventual replacement for CVS. Usable, but as of September 2003 is still alpha quality.

Visual SourceSafe
⇒ `msdn.microsoft.com/ssafe/`
Microsoft's version control offering, so expect good integration with Microsoft tools.

B.4 Bibliography

[BA03] Stephen P. Berczuk and Brad Appleton. *Software Configuration Management Patterns: Effective Teamwork, Practical Integration.* Addison-Wesley, 2003.

[Cla04] Mike Clark. *Pragmatic Automation.* The Pragmatic Programmers, LLC, Raleigh, NC, and Dallas, TX, (planned for) 2004.

[Fog99] Karl Franz Fogel. *Open Source Development with CVS: Learn How to Work With Open Source Software.* The Coriolis Group, third edition, 1999.

[HT03] Andy Hunt and Dave Thomas. *Pragmatic Unit Testing with JUnit.* The Pragmatic Programmers, LLC, Raleigh, NC, and Dallas, TX, 2003.

[Pur00] Gregor N. Purdy. *CVS Pocket Reference.* O'Reilly & Associates, Inc, Sebastopol, CA, 2000.

[Ves03] Jennifer Vesperman. *Essential CVS.* O'Reilly & Associates, Inc, Sebastopol, CA, 2003.

Index

Symbols

A

B

C

D

E

F

N

O

P

Q

R

Pragmatic Starter Kit

Version control. **Unit Testing**. **Project Automation**. Three great titles, one objective. To get you up to speed with the essentials for successful project development. Keep your source under control, your bugs in check, and your process repeatable with these three concise, readable books from The Pragmatic Bookshelf.

Visit Us Online

Version Control Home Page
`pragmaticprogrammer.com/sk/vc`
Source code from this book, errata, and other resources. Come give us feedback, too!

Register for Updates
`pragmaticprogrammer.com/updates`
Be notified when updates and new books become available.

Join the Community
`pragmaticprogrammer.com/community`
Read our weblogs, join our online discussions, participate in our mailing list, interact with our wiki, and benefit from the experience of other Pragmatic Programmers.

New and Noteworthy
`pragmaticprogrammer.com/news`
Check out the latest pragmatic developments in the news.

Save on the PDF

Save over 60% on the PDF version of this book. Owning the paper version of this book entitles you to purchase the PDF version for only $7.50 (regularly $20.00). That's a saving of more than 60%. The PDF is great for carrying around on your laptop. It's hyperlinked, has color, and is fully searchable. Buy it now at `pragmaticprogrammer.com/coupon`

Contact Us

Phone Orders:	1-800-699-PROG (+1 919 847 3884)
Online Orders:	`www.pragmaticprogrammer.com/catalog`
Customer Service:	`orders@pragmaticprogrammer.com`
Non-English Versions:	`translations@pragmaticprogrammer.com`
Pragmatic Teaching:	`academic@pragmaticprogrammer.com`
Author Proposals:	`proposals@pragmaticprogrammer.com`